To
Esther +
Susan

"The story of the
greatest commander of
them all"

Mum
Hadley
"76"

Alexander the Great

Alexander the Great

Frank Lipsius

Introduction by Lord Chalfont

Saturday Review Press
New York

Filmset and printed Offset Litho in Great Britain by Cox & Wyman Ltd, London, Fakenham and Reading

ISBN 0–8715–0331–1 Library of Congress Catalog No 74–408

Saturday Review Press 201 Park Avenue South New York, NY 10003

To the Mills family: home away from home

Contents

Introduction

ALEXANDER THE GREAT first strode on to the stage of military history in 338 BC, when Philip II of Macedonia defeated the Greeks at Chaeronea. During a period of internal dissension in Greece, Macedonia had emerged as a significant military power, and the Greeks had succeeded in forming a coalition of their warring city-states in an attempt to meet this threat to their traditional supremacy. At the battle of Chaeronea, the Macedonians achieved a crushing victory in a confrontation of almost equal forces, in which Philip's son, Alexander, played a decisive part when he massacred the 'Sacred Band' (a battalion of élite Theban troops) on the right flank of the Greek United Armies, and then wheeled behind the Greek lines in a classic cavalry manoeuvre.

With the makeshift coalition of Greek city-states crushed, Alexander, who had succeeded Philip in 336 BC, proclaimed Greek unity and required each of the city-states to provide troops for his Asian operations. There followed, over a period of twelve years, one of the greatest military campaigns in history, as Alexander the Great set out to punish the Persians for their earlier invasions of Greece and to create an empire extending over most of the known world. He defeated the Persians in three great battles at Granicus (334 BC), Issus (333 BC) and Gaugamela (331 BC), and swept on to the frontiers of India where he fought one of his most brilliant battles in 326 BC. This was, however, the last of his great victories. Three years later he died, at the age of thirty-two, in Babylon, and his empire gradually disintegrated.

Technically, the art and science of war had advanced considerably during this period. The main weapon of the Greek city-states was the thrusting spear carried by the *hoplites* or heavy infantrymen, who were formed in compact masses of up to five thousand – the phalanx – which formed the centre of the basic battle formation, with cavalry and light infantry on the flanks and the *psiloi* – special skirmishing forces – out in front. The Athenian armies also had well-organised auxiliary services, including a medical corps of a rudimentary kind. Their tactics were fairly simple, often involving no more than a head-on confrontation between phalanxes.

When Alexander the Great succeeded his father, however, his impact on the military art was dramatic. Tactically he refined the rudimentary but original ideas of Epaminondas of Thebes, developing a system in which the individual phalanx did not advance 'in line' – that is to say in a straight battle front – but roughly in the shape of a V pointing at the enemy. This created a dent in the opposing line and enabled the *hoplites* to pin down the opposing infantry, allowing the cavalry to sweep in on the flanks. The cavalry thus became the decisive arm in battle instead of being used principally as protection for the infantry.

At the same time new engines of war began to make their appearance. The siege tower, the catapult or *ballista*, and the *testudo*, a battering ram under a protective covering of shields. The artillery began to emerge as an organised arm. But the principal factor in the military developments of the era was Alexander the Great himself – one of the greatest generals in history. He showed an extraordinary and precocious skill in combining and manoeuvring forces of all arms; his mastery of tactics was complete and he was able to adapt his method to any form of warfare with which he was confronted, from guerilla warfare to the investing of fortified villages. He was a strategist of remarkable skill and imagination; yet he did not hesitate to lead his own cavalry on the battlefield. Although his basic instincts were aggressive, he never moved on to a new phase in a campaign without first consolidating his gains. In the course of the great twelve-year campaign which took him to the borders of India, he never outran his lines of communication or his administrative support. He brought a new dimension to the military art.

Frank Lipsius tells the story of this remarkable soldier with skill and understanding. It is a story which confirms Field Marshal Montgomery's judgment that, quite apart from Alexander's military genius, his was a great civilising imagination. He was one of the first leaders of the Western world to assert the principle of the brotherhood of mankind, in contrast to the Aristotelian concept of Greece as a civilisation to be kept isolated from contamination by the barbarians of the rest of the world. This is the story of the greatest commander of them all.

Lord Chalfont

7

Preface

HEROIC FIGURES in Greek history before Alexander the Great were apotheosised into gods, some of whose exploits Alexander himself excelled. Though Alexander fostered the development of cults worshipping him as a deity, he fortunately comes down to us as a human being, embellished with romantic and legendary attributes to be sure, but human nevertheless. The job of a biographer is to cut through the romance and put the man back into his historical setting.

For Alexander, such a reappraisal reveals fascinating highlights of the Macedonian court and army but also shows the man as a master intriguer as well as consummate military leader. Historians now suspect Alexander of the murder of his own father, for no longer are we constrained to draw the pat lesson from history that great leadership is virtue incarnate. Alexander definitely participated in the murders of subordinates whose loyalty was never questioned but whose usefulness had ended. He had great visions, but also grave suspicions. The exploits that make us call him 'great' also made him despotic.

As a commander, he has justifiably inspired even the greatest of his military descendants. He met every confrontation with a fresh eye and instinct for the best possible strategy – or strategem. He was daring without being reckless. He trained his men to fight with the precision of a unified military machine. He could also cajole the troops who would have been content to stop before Egypt into following him on to India. Although they later rebelled, we must marvel at the hardships and endless marching that they willingly endured to satisfy his ambition.

Even what is unflattering in a reappraisal of Alexander must still contribute to his reputation and our admiration – at least for his determination. Throughout the ages, Alexander the Great has stood as a measure and challenge to other men's ambitions. It is appropriate that the world still honours him, but even more appropriate that in our own age the achievements of Alexander be measured against the toll exacted in the pursuit of those achievements.

In a superstitious age it might have been considered more than coincidental that my name looks like a misspelling (or latinate form) of Alexander's favourite sculptor, Lysippus. I probably would be as pleased with Alexander's disapprobation of my portrait of him as Lysippus was pleased with his approval. We both, however, have been pursuing the same goal of chiselling Alexander's features as best we can with the tools available to us. My own job has been greatly facilitated by my parents and Elliot Levy, under whose roofs the writing was done; Julie Lipsius and Elaine Elinson for moral support; Dorothy Tomassini, my closest collaborator; and Ian Caruana, my staunchest critic. To them, my thanks for their patience and help.

1 The Court at Pella

I T WAS AN AGE of soldiers of fortune. Bands of mercenaries roamed through Greece and Asia, offering their services to the kings who could afford them. Few could, for Greece had been ravaged by war for almost a century, and though general peace reigned by the mid-fourth century BC, the major powers had adopted defensive postures. The long Peloponnesian War had benefited only the Great King of Persia. The state of demoralisation was such that even Athens, whose proud tradition had for so long been to defend itself unaided, debated for the first time the use of mercenaries.

That Alexander the Great was the world's most successful soldier of fortune tends perhaps to mask the dignity of his achievements. In eight years he marched 11,250 miles from Pella, the Macedonian capital, to beyond the Indus River. He conquered every tribe, every city and empire that he encountered, and was bent on bringing about a new European-Asian fusion of races and government. He did not adopt his contemporaries' condescension towards Asians but respected every native religion and civil practice in the lands through which he passed. Of all conquerors, he could well be assessed as the one most capable of establishing a world order harmonising East and West.

But Alexander was more a soldier than a governor. His challenge was always the army that lay ahead and not the citizens he left behind. Had he lived longer he would undoubtedly have had to face the problem of reconciling the diverse elements of his empire, but his death spared him such domestic worries. He died still confidently dreaming of future conquests. He may have established over seventy Alexandrias, as the Roman historian Plutarch claimed, but most of them were little more than garrisoned communications points. Only one, Alexandria in Egypt, was to maintain prominence beyond the life of its founder, and that was established specifically to replace Tyre (which Alexander had ruthlessly destroyed) as a Middle East trading and commercial centre. When he was cruel and merciless, there was a reason for it; he never hesitated to use intimidation as a weapon when he thought it appropriate. At the same time, he recognised the harm of wanton cruelty, for his was an expedition moving farther and farther into the unknown, depending more and more on the cooperation – or at least the acquiescence – of those behind, farther west. Only a comparatively small force ventured from the Macedonian capital in the spring of 334 BC, but each

PREVIOUS PAGES Macedonia was ringed by mountains on all sides except towards the east, where the river Strymon formed a natural frontier. This view was taken from Amphipolis, captured by Philip II in 357.

OPPOSITE A marble bust of the fourth century BC, thought to be Philip II. Philip belonged to the royal dynasty of the Argeads who claimed descent from Heracles, the son of Zeus.

12

Details from a pebble mosaic from a room, possibly used for dining, at the court at Pella *c.* 300 BC. Hunting was the focal point of a Macedonian's life. Bears and lions roamed the highlands, and elsewhere there were deer in abundance. The scene is thought to depict Alexander (left) being rescued from a lion by Craterus.

15

OPPOSITE The peaks of Olympus, the throne of Zeus and the seat of the gods, were a formidable obstacle for those attempting to invade Greece from the north-east. Their only direct route lay between Olympus and Ossa, through the Vale of Tempe.

conquest brought the tribute, plunder and provisions to finance the next step. Alexander would have happily continued marching into the unknown.

There was ample scope for Alexander's restless energy. The golden age of Athens had been a century earlier. The major cities' strength was sapped, and even the Persian empire felt the effects of having become too bloated and rich with its success. Darius III had been king little longer than Alexander, but whereas the Macedonian had inherited his crown from his father, the Persian owed his to an ambitious and powerful satrap who had already made and then poisoned two other Great Kings of Persia.

Macedonia seemed hardly capable of challenging any of the Greek states, let alone the Persian Empire, which was so rich in gold and manpower. Geographically, Macedonia had the potential for prosperity. Its hills were well supplied with fir trees, necessary for the making of arms and ships. It was a big country, sitting between the city-states of southern Greece and the Persian outposts in Asia Minor. It had played a role in history before, when Xerxes invaded Greece and Alexander's great-grandfather, Alexander I, had treacherously advised the Greeks. But those hills seemed destined to remain as unnoticed by history as the shepherds who tended their flocks there, for the country lacked unity, culture and prosperity, prerequisites that were beyond the reach of such a second-rate kingdom – at least until Philip II, Alexander's father, ascended the throne.

Towards the end of his own life, Alexander the Great rallied his mutinous troops with the memory of his father: 'Philip found you as poor nomads, clothed in sheepskin while you pastured your sparse sheep in the mountains. He gave you cloaks instead of skins, brought you down from the mountains and gave you cities; civilised you with good laws and customs.' It is not the kind of praise Alexander would have indulged in earlier in his life when his father's achievements seemed little more than encroachments on his own ambitions. The words exaggerated past poverty to inflate current prosperity. Still, they did acknowledge the debt that Alexander's accomplishments owed to his father. The groundwork for a world empire had been laid by Philip. The essential ingredients of a stable state, a proven professional army and a continuing source of revenue, were all at

16

A silver coin of Perdiccas III (365-59), Philip II's older brother. On his death Philip assumed the regency of Macedonia until his astonishing career of expansion and conquest forced Amyntas, Perdiccas' son, to give up his claim to the throne.

Alexander's disposal when he undertook the campaign to Asia Minor that his father had planned.

Going back even further, the Argead dynasty had been fortunate more than once in its line of succession. Alexander I, the great-grandfather of Alexander the Great, was a Persian satrap who managed to ingratiate himself with the Greeks. Serving under Xerxes, whose invasion Alexander the Great sought to avenge, he gave information to the Athenians that was later rewarded by his being accepted at the Olympic games as a Hellene. In the next century, Alexander II ruled for only a year but made the significant contribution of creating the Foot Companions. It strengthened the monarchy by balancing the aristocratic power of the Mounted Companions with an honour completely dependent on the king.

Philip's older brother Perdiccas had begun the process of consolidating the kingdom which Philip actually achieved. The independent power of highland nobles was forcibly curtailed. In a battle against the neighbouring Illyrians, however, Perdiccas was killed along with four thousand other Macedonians, leaving the country abjectly vulnerable. Philip became regent for his nephew while outside powers supported alternative client-kings for the Macedonian army's approval. Philip defeated these rivals, secured the throne for himself and, at the age of twenty-four, faced the formidable task of stabilising a disorganised state.

He began by establishing a viable economy. Trade flourished with the three-fingered Chalcidice peninsula just below Macedonia. Timber was shipped in large quantities to Athens. The gold mines at Mount Pangaeum were conquered, providing more than a thousand talents a year to support Philip's ambitions.

Both Philip and Alexander had their contributions to make to the conduct of war. Traditionally the phalanx consisted of eight ranks of soldiers as much as five hundred feet across. The ranks were so close that even the fifth rank, its spears pointed forward, stuck out three feet in front of the first rank, making for a redoubtable hedge of spear points. Philip followed the example of Thebes, where he had been a student and then a hostage for three years. (The period coincided with the height of Theban power under the brilliant leader and strategist Epaminondas, whose father had been host to Philip during his stay.) Philip arranged his phalanx in sixteen ranks twenty-one feet long. Their spears were longer than the traditional ones and the force attacked in a steady advance rather than a charge. The Foot Companions on the left wing had a defensive role while the enlarged Companion cavalry, organised in district squadrons, attacked on the right.

Alexander mobilised the phalanx into a human fortress sixteen men deep and sixteen men across. The spears were reduced to less than two feet in length, but the men fought shoulder to shoulder in such close ranks that the first five ranks still thrust their spears forward, while the remainder rested theirs on the shoulders of the ones in front. Through constant drilling they could form a wedge or V shape on signal and countermarch or make a flanking movement as though they were a solid mass.

A new strategy accompanied the new formation. No longer was the object of victory to place a trophy on the battlefield. Philip chased his enemies in what was an original version of total war. He also pioneered the use of siege machines in eastern Greece after they had been invented in Syracuse. Not content to starve a besieged city, Philip attacked, using his machines against Perinthus and Byzantium. They did not succeed, but their further development into the torsion siege machinery used by Alexander was an invention of significance

LEFT A fourth-century lead sling bullet from Athens.
RIGHT A bronze arrow-head bearing the name of Philip of Macedonia, found at Olynthus – probably for an arrow designed to be fired from a machine.

The departure of a warrior depicted on a red-figure vase from Lucania, *c.* 420, an area of southern Italy where Greek influence was very strong. The shield was usually supported by a thick metal loop to fit over the elbow.

comparable to that of gunpowder, almost a millennium later. Before these machines, city walls were virtually impregnable. Battles took place only in the summer, when growing crops and grazing animals outside the walls made cities vulnerable. Relying on starving a city had been a risky business since the besieging troops were not themselves easily supplied with food. It was a sign of barbarity to the Greek orator Demosthenes, who said against Philip, 'I need not mention that he makes no distinction between summer and winter, that he has no stated season of repose.'

Though he had only ten thousand soldiers, Philip began his career without the use of mercenaries. The ones captured in his early exploits were paroled rather than recruited, a decision that receives the praise of none other than Machiavelli. In fact Machiavelli lavishes as much praise on Philip as he does on Alexander. Where the wiles of leadership

20

are concerned, Philip had proved himself unquestionably. His was the immense task of building Macedonia from a barbaric region into an organised state capable of conquering all Greece. His eschewing mercenaries followed the long practice of the Greek states, which during their heyday would employ no one to defend them. Machiavelli saw the wisdom of this policy because of the mercenaries' loyalty only to money, making them the first to flee in an unsuccessful contest. Machiavelli also lauded Philip's diplomatic ability, which allowed him to appease one enemy while attacking another. Throughout his career Philip had to ensure that alliances were not formed against him. In the early days when Macedonia was at her weakest, he went further than that and mounted his attacks when his enemies were being distracted by other troubles – also instigated by Philip.

Philip soon insinuated himself into Greek politics. He made peace with Athens, then took her former colony of Amphipolis, which protected the gold mines of Mount Pangaeum. He made an alliance with the Chalcidice League, which feared Athens, and was then absorbed by Philip. To distract Athens during this last manoeuvre, he instigated a revolt in an Athenian colony, Euboea. Demosthenes was understandably repelled by Philip's brazen policy of bribing politicians and leaders of the cities on which he had designs. After marriage alliances and the annexing of western

Apollo, the son of Zeus and principal god of prophecy and divination, to whom the oracle at Delphi belonged, wearing a laurel wreath on a gold stater of Philip II. The reverse shows a two-horse chariot which may be connected with Philip's famous victory at Olympia in 356, the year of Alexander's birth.

Thrace, which covered him eastwards towards Asia Minor, Philip had enough security and strength to intervene in the Sacred Wars. These battles over who would control the sacred territory of Delphi had been going on in central Greece for ten years. Philip fought the Phocians several times in the course of the war, and though he suffered defeat and invasion more than once, he did in the end beat them. Their seat on the Amphictyonic Council – which controlled the rites and territory of Delphi – was transferred to him, an honour important for its giving Philip an official voice in Greek affairs.

The introduction of coined money and the Hellenisation of the Macedonian court were signs of Philip's success. Importing Greek intellectuals and architects was a common practice of prosperous non-Greek rulers. It is to this practice that we owe the word 'mausoleum', the first of which was built for Mausolus of Caria, a contemporary of Philip's. Alexander I had himself been host to Euripides, who wrote the *Bacchae* at the Macedonian court. To Philip's court went Aristotle. Greek began to be used in the business of the court, while Philip himself adopted many of the prerogatives of Persian royalty. A staff of slaves, guards and attendants embellished the royal style. Foreign policy became a personal matter of the king's, as in Persia, with all treaties requiring renegotiation at his death. Though the army had to approve the appointment of the Macedonian king, it had little control over him as long as he lived.

There is no telling how much time Philip actually spent at court, but his attention to foreign affairs and delicate juggling of Macedonian interests gave him little time for domestic life. The king was surrounded by a group of intimates with whom he lived, hunted, fought and feasted. The court itself kept up the more ceremonial affairs which were shared by the feudal nobles and their children, known in the Persian way as Royal Pages. Court life was not always tranquil, for Philip had more than one wife – and the one we know of, Olympias, Alexander's mother, had a fiery temper.

Philip became increasingly preoccupied with his growing conflict with Athens – and vice versa. Historically, the Macedonian state acted as a buffer between the urban societies of southern Greece and the more nomadic, warrior tribes which surrounded them. As Macedonia took on the characteristics of civilisation, the buffer became yet another enemy. The organisation of the nomadic societies, with their

A statue thought to be of
Mausolus, satrap of the
Persian province of Caria
in the years 377 to 353.
It was found outside the
north wall of the tomb
erected shortly after his
death by his wife Artemesia.

In the Hellenistic period the major scene of a mosaic took on the characteristics of a framed picture. In this example of a pebble mosaic from Olynthus, destroyed by Philip in 348, Bellerophon, son of Poseidon, is killing the Chimaera who ravaged Lycia.

strict hierarchies suitable for military command and movement, made aggressiveness natural. Athens, which had been militaristic through much of its history, now had to convince its citizens even to defend themselves. In Macedonia, the nobles traditionally shared power with the king, and Philip's ability to dominate them gave him a strongly disciplined army, which he was prepared to use—as was his son.

The conflict with Athens accelerated when Philip's conquests threatened the Athenian grain supply from Asia Minor. Philip's own allies were by now worried about Macedonia's

RIGHT There are about
fifty extant portraits of
Demosthenes, all presumably
going back to one lost Greek
original, of which this is
thought to be a copy.
Demosthenes dreaded the
possibility that Athens
might lose its independence
and used his oratorical
gifts to rouse the city
against Macedonia.

growing power and when they refused to help conquer Athenian colonies in Thrace, he decided to coerce them. But this Macedonian siege of Byzantium and Perinthus failed because Athens came to their support.

Athens's aid of the besieged cities can be attributed to the forceful impact of one eloquent man who had for long perceived the dangers inherent in his own city. It was against Philip that Demosthenes delivered his famous *Philippics*, which were as much intended to arouse Athens as to vilify Philip:

Should anything happen to Philip, Athens in her present frame of mind will soon create another. This one's rise was due less to his own power than to Athenian apathy. . . . It is his motto that every move must be an advance, and ours is that we never get a grip on reality. . . . He knows very well that even with complete control of all the rest he can have no security while democracy remains in Athens, that in the event of a single setback every element under the sway of force will come to Athens for refuge.

But Athens had nonetheless continued to be more influenced by the Peace Party, which was dominated by the young intellectuals of the Academy (including Socrates' nephew) and the notable orator Isocrates. After proposing a general campaign against Persia earlier in his career, Isocrates was ninety when he appealed specifically to Philip to undertake the mission of reconciling the Greek states. Isocrates was also inclined to call Philip a barbarian but the respectability he lent to Philip's ambitions was no doubt greatly appreciated. Philip had no reason to take Isocrates' open letter particularly seriously; indeed its vagueness scarcely warranted it. But here was another instance which Demosthenes so deplored of finding a supporter of Philip within their city's gates, ready to open them to their dire enemy.

In fact, Isocrates may well have been the more realistic of the two great orators. Demosthenes noted several occasions when Philip could have been beaten, but with those opportunities now gone, the incipient weakness of Athens was bound to show up in a confrontation. Indeed, Demosthenes himself pointed to the social decline of Athens, a city no longer inspired to patriotism, willing for the first time to let mercenaries take to the battlefield in place of the citizens. The very rise of oratory has been associated with the decline of a city so recalcitrant and difficult to arouse. Demosthenes could but try:

OPPOSITE The young Alexander with a lion helmet, portrayed as Heracles from whom he claimed descent. The bust is of the fourth century BC and may be by Lysippus.

26

The Lion of Chaeronea
stands guard over the graves
of the Sacred Band who
stood up against the
Macedonians after their
allied army broke and fled.

If, then, this country is prepared to adopt a similar outlook and to break with the past, if every man is ready to take the post which his duty and his abilities demand in service to the state, and set pretences aside, if financial contribution is forthcoming from the well-off and personal service from the appropriate group – in a word if we are prepared to be ourselves, to abandon the hope to evade our duty, we shall recover what is our own, we shall regain what inertia has lost us, and we shall inflict retribution upon Philip.

For all their urgency, it was still another ten years before Athens responded to these strident words.

Philip achieved his conquest of Greece at the battle of Chaeronea in August 338. Finally aroused to concerted effort against the Macedonian army, Athens and Thebes objected to Philip's further interference in affairs of the Amphictyonic Council. Philip had eagerly answered the call of the League to punish one of the states which was said to be cultivating land sacred to Apollo. Athens and Thebes had already refused to administer the punishment and were especially incensed at Philip's planting himself at a strategic crossroads just north of Thebes instead of at the offending city. He called on the Thebans to join him in an attack on Athens, but the Thebans felt safer with Demosthenes' call to join the Athenians against Philip.

The two sides were evenly matched in numbers. The Greek allies held a positional advantage, with their right wing backed against a river and their left extending to the foothills by the town. But the Macedonians had the advantage in experience, for though the Theban 'Sacred Band' were seasoned fighters, the Athenians were novices. Philip's army had already seen a dozen years of war.

The Macedonian strategy was one that was employed extensively throughout Philip's and then Alexander's reign. The offensive and defensive wings of the phalanx gave the Macedonian army a flexibility that could be used to strategic advantage. For instance, the offensive wing of cavalried Companions was on the left here, as opposed to its usual position on the right. More important, Philip directed a closely co-ordinated retreat of his infantry to draw the Athenians into a charge. This broke the ranks of the Greek allied line and allowed the Macedonian cavalry to charge the Theban line. Charging in the gap open at the centre between the Thebans and the Athenians put the Sacred Band on the defensive. Alexander, taking part in this campaign and leading the charge

At the turn of the century
the capital of Macedonia was
moved from Aigai north-east
to Pella, a site more
accessible to the sea. Philip
improved it and within
twenty years of Alexander's
death it could boast elegant
temples and palaces reaped
from the profits of
world-conquest.

through this gap, was treated to the fruits of a spectacular victory which left the Thebans slaughtered at the position where they stood. In their place now stands the huge stone memorial 'Lion of Chaeronea'. In Athens there still exist today graves with legible inscriptions to the dead:

> How striving on Boeotia's storied plain
> To save our sacred Hellas, we were slain.

Plutarch wrote of Philip's unexpected and dramatic victory: 'Some divinely ordained power shaped the course of events to end the freedom of the Greeks.' Demosthenes himself had fought at Chaeronea, but not with honour, for 'he left his place in the ranks and took to his heels in the most shameful fashion, throwing away his arms in order to run faster', relates Plutarch. 'He did not hesitate to disgrace the inscription on his shield, on which was engraved in gold "with good fortune".' When news of the defeat reached Athens, the fear of Philip's wrath and known ruthlessness caused a panic.

The fear was well justified, for in the flush of victory and a drunken revelry Philip gloated over the dead bodies of the enemy left on the battlefield. He also showed his wrath towards the Thebans. Their prisoners were ransomed or sold into slavery. The leaders of the anti-Macedonian faction in Thebes were executed, and an oligarchy was established under Philip's control. The Boeotian League, which Thebes controlled, was dissolved and three towns destroyed by Thebes were ordered to be restored. As a final humiliation, a Macedonian garrison was established in the Theban citadel.

Athens expected the same fate and prepared to resist. But Philip offered surprisingly lenient terms. The Athenian prisoners were returned without ransom. Though Athens had to disband her confederacy, she kept her Aegean possessions and recovered a city from Thebes. She had to become an ally of Macedonia, but Philip agreed not to send troops into Attica or warships to Piraeus. Philip had in fact allowed the defeated armies to retreat from the battlefield without being slaughtered and the bodies of those killed in the battle were returned to Athens for a state funeral, at which Demosthenes delivered the oration.

Philip's overall strategy was to strengthen and restore smaller cities at the expense of the larger ones, which he obviously had greater cause to fear. His real designs were on Asia and the Persian king; so in the full knowledge of victory

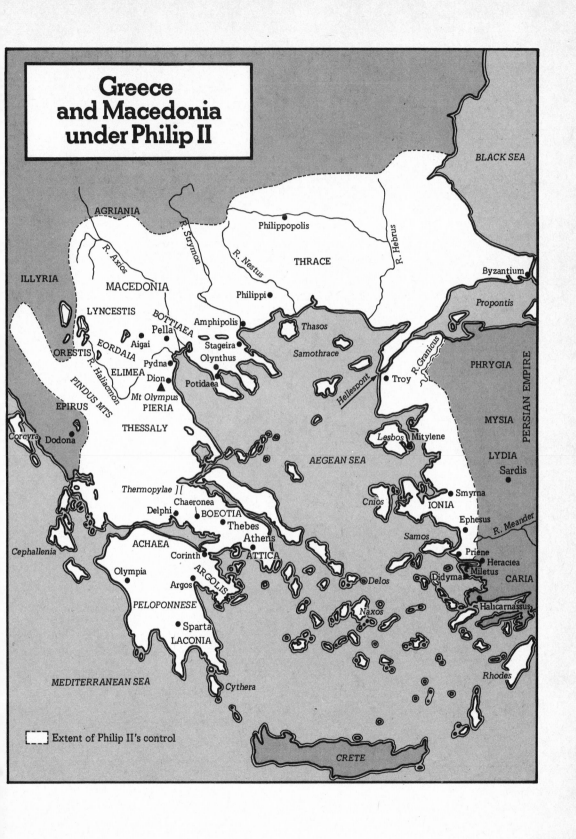

Greece and Macedonia under Philip II

BLACK SEA

AGRIANIA

R. Strymon

Philippopolis

R. Axios

R. Nestus

THRACE

R. Hebrus

ILLYRIA

MACEDONIA

Byzantium

Propontis

LYNCESTIS

BOTTIAEA

Amphipolis

Thasos

R. Granicus

PHRYGIA

EORDAIA

Pella

Philippi

ORESTIS

Aigai

Stageira

Samothrace

PERSIAN EMPIRE

R. Haliacmon

Pydna

Olynthus

Hellespont

Troy

ELIMEA

Dion

Potidaea

MYSIA

PINDUS MTS

Mt Olympus

PIERIA

EPIRUS

THESSALY

Lesbos

Mitylene

LYDIA

Corcyra

Dodona

AEGEAN SEA

Sardis

Smyrna

Thermopylae][

Cnios

IONIA

Chaeronea

Delphi

BOEOTIA

Ephesus

R. Meander

Thebes

Cephallenia

ACHAEA

Athens

Samos

Priene

Corinth

ATTICA

Heraclea

Olympia

ARGOLIS

Delos

Didyma

Miletus

CARIA

Argos

PELOPONNESE

Naxos

Halicarnassus

Sparta

LACONIA

MEDITERRANEAN SEA

Rhodes

Cythera

Extent of Philip II's control

CRETE

he made a great display of leniency and statesmanship. The Greeks still harboured fears of this northern barbarian who had conspicuously connived, threatened and invaded the peace of Greece. He now showed a more benign side, which was greeted with as much appreciation as surprise.

For his leniency towards them, the Athenians made Philip and Alexander (who escorted the ashes of the slain Athenians back to Athens) honorary citizens and even proposed putting up a statue of Philip in the market place. In central Greece, Philip arranged for the penalty against the defeated Phocians to be reduced from sixty talents a year to ten. A statue of Philip was erected at Delphi.

Philip then led the Macedonian army on a peaceful march through the Peloponnese where he was honoured by all the states except Sparta, which denied the army entry. Philip arbitrated various territorial disputes and notably made over some of Sparta's land to the Arcadian League, which he had encouraged to re-form to balance Sparta's power. At the same time he invited the Greek states to come to a meeting in the autumn, meanwhile withdrawing to Macedonia.

Late in 338 Philip called the Peace Congress at Corinth, which crowned his political power over Greece. His controlling influence brought peace to Greece and gave him scope for his further ambitions. He was technically not a member of the pact since Macedonia was not considered one of the Greek city-states, but he so engineered the conference that the peace suited his designs. The Greek cities were entitled to control their own domestic affairs, though he had already placed allies of his own in charge of numerous governments. He was also allowed to keep his garrisons stationed at Thebes, Chalcis, Corinth and Ambracia.

The pact made provision for a *hegemon* – a less objectionable name than 'king' – which gave Philip considerable latitude to interfere in Greek affairs. He alone made external policy and carried it out for Greece. Disputes between states in Greece were to be settled by the League's own council, composed of representatives from all the states. But both parties had to agree to arbitration, and if they didn't Philip had the power to intervene arbitrarily.

For the larger Greek cities it was a humiliating blow. Demosthenes told his Athens audience, 'We have been the leaders of Greece for seventy-three years and Sparta for twenty-nine. Thebes gained some power recently after the battle of Leutra. But never was Athens, Thebes or Sparta given such power – never by a long way.' Since Philip could have destroyed Athens and his other former enemies, there were some who could speak of Philip's generosity, though of course his Asian plans required the acquiescence of Greece in general and the use of Athens's navy in particular.

It is probably true, moreover, that the Greek cities could not have themselves achieved the peace that Philip gave them. There had been a justifiable fear that Philip's ambitions would cause Greek governments to be destroyed, but they carried on. At this very time Aristotle was writing about the democracy of the Athenian city-state in the words that we use to describe it today. The League lasted throughout the reign of Alexander, during which Antipater – the regent in Macedonia – acted as hegemon. As Philip had planned, the League provided some troops for the expedition, but they were more like hostages than allies, for Alexander was his father's son and knew how to exploit the advantages he inherited.

2
The
Great
Competitor

MYTH LARGELY REPLACES FACT in our knowledge of the young Alexander. The Greeks invoked myths where we would call on psychology. No particular attention was paid to a child, except to assure that he was educated to fill his station in life, his upbringing being a matter of political as well as personal considerations. And so when Alexander reached his maturity and achieved what he did, the coincidences and circumstances of his birth and early years took on a patina of legend that disguise the inability to account rationally for his particular genius.

Alexander's mother was a princess with a fiery temper named Olympias. Marriage to her had political importance for Philip since it cemented peace with the fierce neighbours of Epirus, but the two were also said to have met and fallen deeply in love while attending a religious ceremony on the island of Samothrace. The ceremony initiated them into the mysteries of the Cabiri, twin gods who promoted fertility and protected sailors. At the time of Philip and Olympias' romance the gods were associated with Dionysus, but with the birth of their son, the cult soon spread throughout the Greek world and became associated with Alexander.

Olympias, at the time of her marriage, was given to keeping live snakes as pets. They were used in the wildest forms of religion, which she practised. A worshipper of Dionysus, the god of Nature's vitality, she participated in the orgiastic celebrations which culminated in the sacrifice of a lamb or – in extreme but known cases – a human being. Philip was then regent in Macedonia. Though only twenty-one, he had been married twice. Both his wives had died in 357, the same year he married Olympias.

The myths abound. Olympias' womb was said to have been struck by lightning; some held that she was violated by Zeus in the form of a snake, others that her body was sealed and guarded by a lion. The soothsayers were at first nonplussed by such signs, interpreting them to mean that Philip had better keep an eye on his wife. Aristander of Telmessus, who was to be part of Alexander's entourage for the duration of his reign, made his auspicious start here, at Alexander's birth. It was Aristander's conviction that the gods were signifying the greatness of Philip's offspring.

Philip was off in battle when Alexander was born in the summer of 356. It is said that as he rested from his own victory, a messenger came with news that the Macedonian

38

RIGHT A maenad on a red-figure vase depicting Dionysiac revels, not unlike the ones Olympias took part in. Adorned with skins and wreaths of ivy, oak and fir, the maenads were idealised versions of the 'frenzied women' who participated in the god's orgies.

BELOW Zeus giving birth to Athena from his head. Alexander styled himself as the descendant of both Zeus and Achilles. On his way to meet Darius he honoured Athena at Troy, taking in return a set of weapons dating back to the Trojan war – as Achilles had once done.

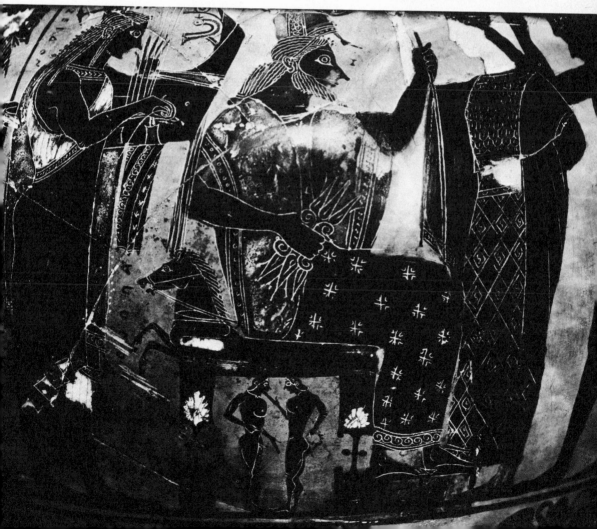

general Parmenio had just won his battle. Then another messenger arrived to report that a horse of Philip's had just won in the Olympics. And finally a third messenger galloped up with the climactic news that a son had been born to Olympias. One other coincidental event was grafted on to the same day – the burning of the temple at Ephesus in Asia Minor, which Alexander later offered to rebuild. For now, it was interpreted as a recognition by the gods of the day's cataclysmic birth.

At court, Alexander was raised very much as the son of the king and as heir presumptive to the Macedonian crown. The position of his mother, being a foreigner, was less secure than his own, though part of the attention lavished on him reflected the campaign to assure his loyalty to Macedonia and its social structure. He was nursed by the sister of Cleitus, who was commander of the Royal Squadron of the Companion cavalry, and thus one of Philip's most trusted nobles. Olympias countered the influence of the court with foreign teachers for her son. One of them was a kinsman of hers and he was assisted by a better-known foreigner, Lysimachus, a lenient master who later accompanied Alexander into Asia.

The child's lessons included Homer, the *Iliad* being a text that Alexander valued and carried throughout his life. Lysimachus' apparent fancy was to pretend that Alexander was Achilles, while he himself was Phoenix, Achilles' teacher. Since Olympias claimed descent from Achilles, Alexander is thought to have taken the parallels seriously. Alexander showed little interest in athletics, though he was an excellent runner. When he was encouraged to compete in the Olympic games, he said haughtily he would race 'only against other kings'. Besides learning to read and write, he was taught how to play the lyre. Normal training would take in the sword, the bow and the javelin. Riding he learned in childhood, his disciplining of Bucephalus being an early example of his skill. This horse who carried Alexander into Asia was given to him only because he was able to master it as a young teenager. The horse's wildness made the trained riders keep away from him. Alexander, having noticed that the horse's shying came from his own shadow, brazenly challenged his father to let him attempt what the adults couldn't do. Philip expressed some annoyance at what he took to be youthful arrogance and made Alexander wager

LEFT A bronze statue of the young Alexander wearing the goatskin *aegis* traditionally associated with Zeus and Athena. It was adopted by the Macedonian Argead dynasty as an emblem of royalty.

41

the extraordinary price of the horse against his own
boast. Alexander took the bet. He led the horse into the
sun to avoid the shadow, calming the animal the while by
stroking it reassuringly. He then lightly leaped on to its back,
still encouraging its steps, until Bucephalus was prepared to
have full rein, all of this much to the amazement of those
watching. According to Plutarch, who tells this story, Philip
wept for joy and told Alexander, 'Son, you must find a kingdom big enough for your ambitions. Macedonia is too small
for you.'

Philip arranged for Alexander to be taught by Aristotle
for three years, beginning when the boy was thirteen.
Aristotle had not yet established his school in Athens, as he
was to do while his pupil was marching through Asia, but
he had already studied with Plato for twenty years and had
spent time studying marine biology in Asia Minor. These
major influences behind him when he came to Pella, Aristotle
had no doubt reached his maturity, though not yet his
universal fame.

Alexander accompanied Aristotle to a retreat at Mieza,
where a number of the Macedonian court children joined
them for their studies. Hephaestion, Alexander's lifelong
companion and confidant, was probably among the group.
The appointing of Aristotle, enlightened as it may appear,
was probably done for political rather than academic reasons.
Aristotle himself was born in an area controlled by Philip.
The philosopher's father-in-law was a Persian satrap in Asia
Minor who had already collaborated with the Greeks against
his master, the Persian king. Philip obviously saw the
benefit of ingratiating himself with the satrap, but to no avail,
since the Persian king eventually found out about the
betrayal and the satrap was killed. Philip had to settle for the
single advantage of getting one of history's most celebrated
thinkers as tutor for his son.

We do not know what transpired between master and
pupil. Much has been made of the contact between the age's
greatest conqueror and greatest mind, but both men's major
achievements lay ahead of them. Moreover, Alexander was
just an adolescent, being taught among a group of friends in
a congenial setting.

But neither should this period be dismissed. There are
stories of Alexander's precocious and worldly outlook when
he was no more than seven years old, half the age at which

OPPOSITE A bronze statuette
of Alexander taming
Bucephalus, probably
Hellenistic–Etruscan,
c. fourth century BC.

42

Aristotle was assigned with his students to the lowland town of Mieza, a village in the eastern foothills of the Bernius range, north of Beroea. This precinct probably formed part of the famous 'Garden of Midas', a district of fine vineyards and orchards.

he was Aristotle's pupil. The best known of the stories claims that the young Alexander met envoys from Persia and instead of asking juvenile questions, wanted pertinent information about the character of the Great King, the empire's military strength, the distance between major cities and the Persian terrain. And for Alexander, this period under Aristotle was also his last academic training before he became involved in the politics of Macedonia.

Aristotle's major interests were marine biology and politics. Of the former, Alexander was to send the master specimens and information throughout his expedition. Alexander confirmed Aristotle's belief that the Caspian Sea was not the bay of some northern ocean, which the Greeks had thought bordered the world. In Egypt, Alexander sent a group to find out why the Nile overflowed in summer. The answer was that there were summer rains in the Abyssinian moun-

44

tains, from which information Aristotle noted triumphantly that 'this is no longer a problem'.

In politics Aristotle made the first comparative study of governments. We do not know how much of this knowledge he imparted to his pupils. It certainly would have been valuable and Alexander was no doubt capable of absorbing it. It also deserves some elaboration, if only to give an idea of the political thinking of the times and the kind of counsel that a king – or prince – would get to encourage him in good government.

There was an important distinction between kings and tyrants. 'The tyrant's aim is pleasure; the king's is duty. Hence they differ in their appetites and ambitions: the tyrant grasps at money, the king at honour. A king's bodyguard is made up of citizens, a tyrant's of mercenaries.' There was the recognition that societies are more than a collection of individuals, for 'the state is more than an investment; its purpose is not merely to provide a living but to make a life that is worthwhile'.

In summary form, these ideas sound like glib maxims of good government, but at the time they had significance in distinguishing one form of government from another and creating limits on the arbitrary power of kings. Aristotle went so far as to justify absolute power in the hands of the right ruler, the one who shows his 'superiority in some form of goodness'. So it was not so much the form of government that made a difference as the quality of leader exercising the power. Such a concept, so alien to our own reliance on the form of government as the foundation of legitimacy, resulted from philosophers' access to kings, who theoretically could be persuaded to adopt the right policies. If Aristotle had more influence over a king than over a public, democratic meeting, then he had reason to believe that the king would perform his duties better than the democracy would. In Athens there were numerous instances to be found of a democracy being subverted by demagogues or passionate responses to issues, which Aristotle deplored as much as despotism.

An area of particular interest to Alexander would have been Aristotle's lessons on the difficulty of turning a militaristic state into a peaceful one. The master was explicit about the dangers involved, given the example of Sparta: 'The military states generally, while they fight wars, survive,

Alexander the Great, probably the work of Leochares, c. 330 BC.

but once they establish an empire begin to decline. Like steel they lose their fine temper if they are always at peace.' Alexander never lived to see the conclusion of his military ambitions, but he did have to contend with the governments of states as he conquered them. He struck upon the appropriate formula only midway through Asia Minor, after which he gradually moved towards a simple alternative of either retaining the previous ruler or destroying the capital city. Arbitrary as this sounds, it took courage to trust recent enemies, especially when he could have left his own Companions or bodyguards as a small invasionary force. Instead his Macedonian officials were primarily called upon to collect tax and tribute. The satrap of Babylon, for instance, was confirmed in his position within a week of leading a Persian attack against Alexander in the battle of Gaugamela. He was even allowed to retain the coveted right to coin money, but then Alexander always admired a courageous fighter, as this satrap Mazaeus was.

Some of this leniency and privilege showed instincts and policy that Alexander could not have learned from Aristotle. The king was willing to treat Asians as equals and to respect not only their religion and local customs but also the governors who were willing to cooperate. Alexander's conquests could not have extended as far as they did had he shared Aristotle's prejudice against Asians. The lenience and toleration, whether stemming initially from convenience or personal inclination, eventually evolved into a conscious policy to fuse races into a new European-Asian people, united in their loyalty to an empire of unprecedented size. The extent to which Alexander intended to pursue this policy cannot be known, since he died before he had the chance to implement it, but we might reasonably suppose that the plan to govern an empire existed in Alexander's mind from the time of Aristotle's salutory lessons, long before the need arose.

In 340, at the age of sixteen, Alexander graduated direct from his studies to appointment as regent in Macedonia while his father was away besieging the recalcitrant cities Byzantium and Perinthus (see chapter 1). By now he was assumed to be an adult; besides his new responsibilities, he was sculpted for the first time in a bust attributed to Leochares, who portrayed the features that were to be reproduced many times during and after Alexander's lifetime. He

46

had large eyes, long cheeks and a rounded chin. He wa
described as having a fierce, lion-like countenance, with
prominent bridge to a nose whose sharp verticality gave him
something of a boxer's pugnacious look. Though short, h
made an imposing figure, in contrast to his father, who looked
impressive because he was tall, dark-haired and one-eyed (a
the result of a battle injury). Philip was not merely extending
Alexander's education by making him regent and keeper of the
royal seal. He had need of a kinsman in a responsible position
for power given to another nobleman detracted from the
king's own independence.

Even as regent at his tender age, Alexander found a battle o
his own when he couldn't join his father's. His first fighting
experience was in a campaign he himself devised. While
Philip was besieging the two cities, a Thracian tribe revolted
thinking Alexander could not mount a battle against them
In response he acted decisively, organising troops with the
help of the noble, Antipater, and setting out to subdue the
tribe. He turned their city into a Macedonian garrison, which
he named Alexandropolis in imitation of his father'
Philippolis, the garrison that guarded the gold mines o
Mount Pangaeum, not far from Amphipolis.

Alexander was more successful than his father who, it wil
be recalled, had to abandon the siege because of Athens's help
to the two cities. As a means of replenishing his depleted
treasury with booty and giving his troops a morale-boosting
victory, Philip decided to conquer the Scythians on the
Danube. Alexander joined this campaign, in which the
Scythians were easily defeated and deprived of substantia
treasure. But on their return to Macedonia the Triballian
refused the army free passage through their territory. In
the battle to get through, Philip was seriously injured in the
thigh, and much of the booty was lost. It was, however, the
final proving ground for the young Alexander. The next yea
he led the charge in the battle of Chaeronea when Athens and
Thebes were forced to acknowledge the suzerainty of Macedonia. This is the battle where Alexander decimated the
Theban Sacred Band and was also given the privilege of
accompanying the corpses of the thousand Athenian dead
back to Athens.

It was Alexander's only glimpse of the city of which he
must have heard a great deal from Aristotle. It was also
tribute from Philip that he allowed his son to make the

A Hellenistic Greek onyx cameo
of the third century BC, thought
to represent Alexander and Olympias.
Olympias was from the Molossian
House of Epirus, which claimed
descent from Achilles.

49

To commemorate his victory at Chaeronea Philip built and dedicated at Olympia a circular edifice, the Philippeion, for which Leochares was commissioned to make portrait-statues in gold and ivory of the Macedonian royal family.

journey, he himself receiving accolades from the city for his leniency towards them. This climax to Philip's conquest of Greece was also the high point of his relationship with his son. On the battlefield Alexander had been given every opportunity to display his precocious abilities and he had done so admirably, no doubt much to the satisfaction of his father. The troubles between them started only now, when peace brought Philip back to the court with all its intrigues and jockeying for proximity to the great conqueror. Philip's mind was already on the next step – creation of the League of Corinth to legitimise his invasion of Asia. For this new ambition he needed the full cooperation of his nobles, who would be leading the Macedonian troops into new territory.

For their part, the nobles knew that despite Philip's growing power, they too were becoming more important because he needed their support. An unanticipated source of trouble soon arose. As the son of a foreign mother, Alexander even now did not enjoy the wholehearted confidence of the Macedonian nobility. In particular, it seems that Attalus, one of the more influential nobles, was encouraging Philip to find a Macedonian wife to sire an heir to the throne. Attalus had a personal stake in this intrigue, for his niece Cleopatra was the one chosen to be Philip's Macedonian wife. Historians have tended to assert that an overwhelming passion overcame Philip, a conclusion drawn from the folly of Philip's sudden willingness to estrange his son Alexander, now that he had been shown such favour.

The antagonism between father and son came into the open during the celebration accompanying Philip's marriage to Cleopatra. In the midst of the drunken feast Attalus proposed

A mosaic from Baalbek on the Damascus-Emesa caravan route depicting Philip, Olympias and Alexander. Like all such mosaics, this is probably based on a well-known painting.

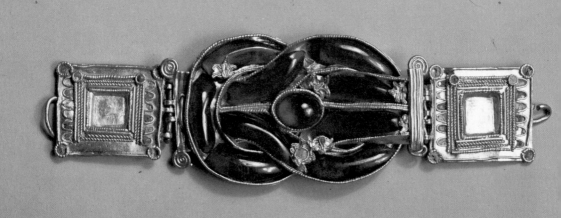

a toast that his niece and Philip give Macedonia a legitimate king. In uninhibited drunken anger, Alexander screamed out to Attalus, 'Do you mean that I'm a bastard?' and threw a goblet at him. Attalus threw one back. Philip, drunk as the rest, took out his sword to attack Alexander! It was a shocking demonstration, even if he had no intention of hurting his son.

Alexander mocked the sight of his father, sword drawn, trying to cross the room to attack him. When his father stumbled and was easily restrained, he called out, 'So this is the man who intends to cross into Asia. He can't even cross the room!' Alexander and Olympias immediately fled from Pella. Alexander accompanied his mother to her home in Epirus and then went to Illyria.

In their absence plans for the invasion of Asia proceeded rapidly. Philip's second in command, Parmenio, was sent with ten thousand troops to Asia Minor where they had great initial success. They conquered several cities while the Greek city of Ephesus turned itself spontaneously over to the Macedonians. In the same year Darius III became the Great King of Persia, but in circumstances of squalid intrigues and confusion which were not altogether clear but certainly bode well for enemies like Macedonia.

Olympias and Philip were by now irreconcilable, but Alexander did return to Pella when an intermediary arranged it. Alexander, though, never lost his suspicion of his father, and the bad blood between them soon became all too apparent; Philip arranged a marriage for his half-witted son Arrhidaeus with the daughter of an Asia-Minor ruler, who had nominally owed allegiance to the Persian king. When Alexander heard of this arrangement, he immediately concluded that a half-brother of his was assuming his place; so he offered himself for the marriage – all behind Philip's back. The king was furious when he found out about Alexander's presumption, which had been completely misguided because in fact Philip would not settle for such a minor match for Alexander. As a result, Alexander's colleagues who had advised him were exiled, leaving the prince isolated in what he continued to believe was a hostile court.

The climactic event did not take long to materialise. Philip arranged for his daughter, also named Cleopatra, to marry Olympias' brother, Alexander of Epirus. Philip had already befriended his brother-in-law by making him king of Epirus. Though Cleopatra was this Alexander's own niece (her

Hellenistic jewellery, late fourth to second century BC: ABOVE A necklace and bracelet; the latter is of Persian origin, though adored by Hellenistic women who usually wore two at once. BELOW A decoration, probably from a diadem, known as a Heracles knot. It was thought to ward off evil.

53

mother was Olympias), the match was a considerable compliment to him and would cement the friendship with Philip despite his estrangement from Olympias. In those days such an alliance would be the one valid hindrance to Olympias' family seeking revenge on Philip for discarding her and eliminating her importance in the Macedonian court.

A splendid wedding was arranged to which Olympias had to be invited. Held in midsummer 336, the ceremony was accompanied by elaborate games and 'gorgeous sacrifices to the gods', as our sources tell us. It was quite a time of celebration for Philip, with his troops showing great success in Asia Minor and his own departure imminent. Moreover, during the preparations for the wedding his wife Cleopatra delivered a son and heir, with the same propitious timing that had accompanied the birth of Alexander.

The day devoted to games began with a dawn procession of the statues of the gods into the stadium. Philip had a statue of himself added to the group, while he followed behind, escorted by his son Alexander and the bridegroom. The bodyguards were kept at a distance, lest Philip appear afraid for his life on the day that he exalted himself level with the gods. He approached the gate of the stadium slowly. Suddenly one of the bodyguards rushed forward. As he ran, he pulled from his tunic a short hunting knife. Reaching Philip he thrust the knife deep into the king's back. Philip died instantly while the slayer turned and fled in the mêlée.

He eluded his pursuers until, getting on to his waiting horse, he tripped over a vine; whereupon the rest of the bodyguards fell upon him with javelins, saving him from gruesome torture. But he was dead before any information could be got out of him about the other plotters in the regicide. The assassin, a man named Pausanias, had as a bodyguard shared the honour of being one of the seven men closest to the king. The question arises not only of why he did it but why he did it now in full public view.

Aristotle gives the only contemporary account still extant. Pausanias apparently had a grudge against Philip hinging on homosexual relations at court, in which Philip participated along with the bodyguards and nobles. The grudge as described is convoluted without directly involving Philip. Pausanias wanted revenge on Attalus for some sexual transgression, and since Attalus was away in Asia Minor, Pausanias chose Philip as his victim. There is reason not to trust

54

Aristotle completely, for had there been a political motive – as we must suspect there probably was – he would surely have wished to protect one prime suspect – his former pupil.

Certainly Alexander had reason to fear the developments in Macedonia, where his favoured position was quickly being eroded. The birth of a Macedonian son to Philip could well have capped his anxiety and his mother's, who was for the moment at court. Mother and son had shown a loyalty to each other that excluded Philip. Either with Alexander, or conceivably on his behalf but without his cooperation, Olympias and Pausanias had quickly hatched and executed their conspiracy. Pausanias was from an area of western Macedonia that Philip had taken from Epirus, Olympias' home. They were sure to have known each other and possibly shared the distress at Olympias' and Alexander's increasing estrangement from the court. It may all be coincidental but then again, there was no hesitation in Alexander's reaching for his father's place. He was now king of Macedonia; he would soon be on his own way to Asia.

3
Auguries of
Success

ALEXANDER WAS IMMEDIATELY PRESENTED to the Macedonian army and proclaimed king. To the dignitaries who had come for a wedding and stayed for a funeral, he promised to carry on the programme of his father. For the Macedonians he eliminated taxes, leaving booty and gold mines as his sources of revenue. It was an impressive show for a twenty-year-old who might normally have expected to languish for most of his life in the shadow of an illustrious father.

The swift transition occurred before Parmenio and his Macedonian army in Asia knew of Philip's death. Alexander was presented to the troops at home by Antipater, the only noble who ranked as high as Parmenio. There was no news of the Asian army's reaction to Alexander's acclamation, a procedure that was supposed to be followed in the presence of the whole army. For the moment Alexander had more immediate problems than his own troops that far away. After some ferreting about, three brothers from Lyncestis, a Macedonian province in the northern hills, were accused of plotting the regicide with Pausanias. Two were executed; the third, a son-in-law of Antipater, was saved, allegedly because he was so quick to accept Alexander as king. Being Antipater's son-in-law was no doubt of greater consequence.

Greece went wild in celebration. Ambracia expelled its Macedonian garrison. Thessaly was taken over by the anti-Macedonian party. Aetolia recalled the exiles whom Philip had banished. Thebes led central Greece in plans to revolt. In Athens, Demosthenes had advance secret news of the murder. He immediately changed from his mourning attire for a daughter who had just died and ran to the Assembly with the good news. He did not say outright that Philip had been murdered, but only that he had dreamed of a great stroke of luck for Athens. When the messenger then ran in with the official word of Philip's death, pandemonium broke loose. A crown was voted for Philip's assassin and sacrifices were immediately offered for the deliverance of Athens. The citizens, including Demosthenes, celebrated, festooned in garlands.

Athens's excessive joy gets a stern rebuke from a moralist like Plutarch, who admired Philip's accomplishments. Besides, says Plutarch, 'it was contemptible to make Philip a citizen of Athens and pay him honours while he was alive, and then, as soon as he had been killed, to be beside themselves with joy,

PREVIOUS PAGES The Temple of Apollo at Delphi. Apollo founded his oracular shrine on the spot where he killed the female serpent Python and named his priestess after her. It was the most important oracle of the Greek world.

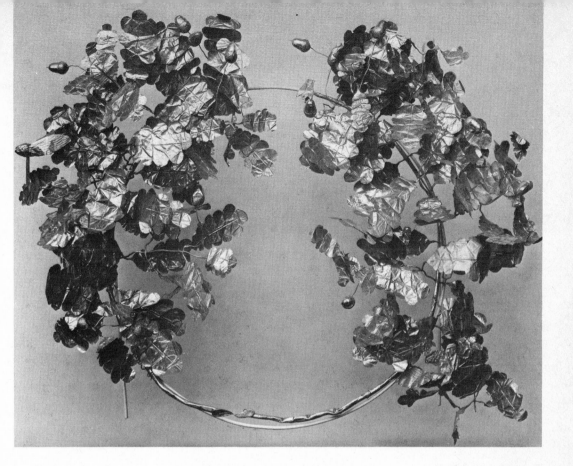

A gold wreath from the Dardenelles of the fourth century BC.

trample his body and sing paeans of victory, as though they themselves had accomplished some great feat. On the other hand, I praise the behaviour of Demosthenes for leaving his personal misfortunes to be lamented by women and devoting himself to the action he thought necessary for his country.'

There was now evidence that Alexander's own troops in Asia Minor were plotting with the Greek rebels. Attalus, who had insulted Alexander at Philip's marriage with Cleopatra, was second in command of the Asia Minor expedition. He corresponded with Demosthenes in Athens and encouraged rebellion. When no uprising followed, Attalus tried to ingratiate himself again with Alexander by forwarding Demosthenes' treasonous correspondence to Pella. Though Attalus was Parmenio's son-in-law, Alexander was so suspicious of him that he risked Parmenio's disloyalty by demanding that the second in command be put to death. Parmenio's agreeing to Alexander's demand averted a possible battle that could then and there have ended Alexander's ambition. No doubt the king carefully calculated his position before making the demand, although his implacable hatred of Attalus probably

59

made him blind to much, including the general's popularity. Indeed Attalus' death was not the only sacrifice made to Alexander's security. Amyntas, the nephew whom Philip had replaced as king, had remained part of the Pella court throughout his childhood. He was a few years older than Alexander and there was some concern that mutinous elements at court might now rally round the hitherto unambitious young man. So he too was killed.

The family of Cleopatra, Philip's 'legitimate' heirs, according to Attalus' offensive toast at their wedding, were also killed. Olympias personally murdered Cleopatra and her infant daughter. Though Alexander piously deplored the murders, he had male members of Cleopatra's family killed to prevent any reprisals on the royal family.

Since political assassination was an accepted practice at that time, Alexander's actions showed less brutality than precaution. Once the sequence of killings began with Philip's murder, it had to be carried through as much for the safety of the state as for the immediate beneficiaries of the regicide.

Though Alexander was at last fully accepted as the legitimate Macedonian ruler, his advisers thought the young king ought to proceed cautiously in assuming the authority of his father. They advised him to concentrate on securing the northern borders of Macedonia and let the Greek states go for the time being. With decisiveness – and at the time seeming recklessness – he rejected any show of acquiescence and decided to march straightaway to regain his father's direct control over Greece. Since the Peace of Corinth gave Philip's successors the right to claim his title as hegemon of the League, Alexander undertook his mission with the confidence of a rightful ruler disciplining rebelliousness.

Though the Greek states had made no concerted opposition to Philip until it was too late, all the states did share unanimous distrust and dislike of the scheme to use Greek support for Macedonian conquests in Asia. There was a real threat that they would band together to expel Alexander from Greek affairs.

The closest of the Greek states was Thessaly. Alexander arrived there by forced march, much to the surprise of the Thessalians guarding the pass at Tempe. While the natives deliberated on whether to admit the Macedonian army through the pass, Alexander had his engineers build steps up the coastal face of Mount Ossa. Having thus circumvented the

A Greek warrior from the
'Amazon Sarcophagus' from
Tarquinia, Etruscan of the
late fourth century BC.

The Vale of Tempe was protected by a pass five miles long and so narrow that the cavalry could only pass through in single file.

pass, he was quick to get himself proclaimed archon of Thessaly in succession to his father. The Thessalian cavalry, which now joined Alexander's forces, played a major part in the king's battles throughout Asia.

In quick succession the other states acknowledged Alexander's suzerainty in Greece. Though at every step ready to fight for his position, at no time did he have to. Even the recalcitrant Thebans sued for peace when Alexander encamped his troops in full battle order outside their walls. By now the Athenians realised that Demosthenes had sorely underestimated the capacity and resolution of the young king. They sent envoys to apologise for not recognising Alexander sooner. At a new meeting of the League of Corinth, Alexander was officially confirmed as Philip's successor, and the resolution to fight against the Persians was renewed.

During the meeting at Corinth a number of distinguished men of Greece came to meet Alexander and offer their congratulations. Diogenes, the eccentric philosopher who lived in a barrel and used a lantern to look for an honest man, was an exception who would not consort with kings. Instead, according to Plutarch, Alexander made a pilgrimage to see Diogenes, then living in Corinth. The philosopher was sunbathing at the time and would not get up to greet his unexpected guest. When Alexander asked if he could do anything for him, he retorted with his legendary, 'Yes, you can get out of my light.' To Alexander's credit he admired the plucky old man and later remarked to his followers that if he were not Alexander, he would have liked to be Diogenes.

Though his sights were set eagerly on Asia, Alexander realised the need to secure his northern boundary before venturing overseas. So the following spring he marched his army towards the tribes living near the Danube. He had been this way before when as regent he had quelled a rebellion on his own inexperienced initiative. The project now was much more ambitious and dangerous. Alexander was determined to push the Macedonian borders beyond the Danube by defeating the tribes on the northern edge of the country. Unlike the battles in Greece, here the fighting resembled guerilla warfare with the enemy having no fixed point of defence and a natural advantage in picking its own time and place of battle. The first encounter proved just how formidable this opposition could be. A tribe of Triballians held a strategic mountain pass which the Macedonian army was approaching from below. At their

63

commanding position the Triballians had assembled wagons which they intended merely to roll downhill as the Macedonian army advanced. Alexander foresaw their intention and designed an intricate manoeuvre to thwart it. To be used again to defeat the king of Persia four years later, here the plan showed just how innovative and authoritative Alexander could be.

Some of his men lay down and put their shields over their heads to deflect the wagons. The rest of his phalanx divided at a signal so the wagons could pass between the ranks unimpeded. With this complicated, coordinated defence, the army escaped with no casualties. When the enemy saw Alexander's army emerge unscathed from their attack they fled in confusion, the Macedonians in hot pursuit. Fifteen hundred of the enemy were killed, but few captured, since they were too quick and knew the country too well to be taken.

Alexander's army next encountered a native force of Triballians near the Danube, protecting themselves in a naturally defensible position. He ordered the phalanx to attack with archers and slingers at the head of the column, advancing at the double. The missiles drew the enemy out to engage the lightly armed archers. Then Philotas led the Macedonian cavalry in a charge in which three thousand of the enemy were killed.

The Triballian populace had meanwhile been directed by their king to flee and take refuge on an island with high embankments in the middle of the swift current of the Danube. Before he left Pella, Alexander had had the foresight to send a fleet from Byzantium to meet the army on the Danube. The ships, however, were ineffectual against the Triballian island stronghold, so Alexander decided instead to cross the Danube and fight the troops of another tribe, the Getae, who had been massing opposite the Macedonian encampment.

The island attempt had proved impossible and this new scheme looked no more feasible, the intention being to cross the Danube in one night and surprise the army with a daybreak attack on the other side. How Alexander managed to transport his fifteen hundred cavalry and four thousand infantry across the Danube so quickly is not altogether clear. He certainly used ingenuity and makeshift resources including dug-out fishing canoes and rafts composed of tents stuffed with hay.

The army landed in high cornfields on the other side.

Greek warriors bid farewell to their womenfolk before setting out for battle.

65

Alexander had the troops assemble and march in formation with spears parallel to the ground to clear the fields in front of them as they went. The cavalry followed the infantry as they moved down the fields, then moved forward to the left wing when Alexander took command. At dawn, on a signal from Alexander, the Macedonians made a loud din clattering their armour. The awesome sound and sight sent the sleepy troops scuttling in full flight four miles back to their settlement beyond the river bank. The Macedonian troops followed cautiously from the river. When it was obvious that Alexander was taking no chances in his methodical advance, the Getae simply abandoned the encampment as quickly as they could and dispersed. The Macedonian troops took over their settlement, which they looted and destroyed.

Alexander received envoys from the Triballians and other tribes along the Danube, all suing for peace. Even the formidable Celts, who were not directly threatened by Alexander, sent envoys. Alexander asked them what they feared most, hoping the tall and powerful Celts would answer that he, Alexander, was what most frightened them. But they said their greatest fear was that the sky would fall in on them, to which the disappointed Alexander replied that the Celts thought too much of themselves. Overall the expedition proved to be a stunning success. There would be peace along the northern border for fifty years, and the collapse of opposition now came just in time to free Alexander for the crisis that suddenly blew up on the western Macedonian border.

All of Illyria seemed to be in revolt. The Illyrian chiefs, Glaucias and Cleitus, were bringing their forces together at Pellion, a Macedonian fortress on the western border, when Alexander heard of their concerted revolt. He marched his troops as fast as possible to Pellion to get there before Glaucias. This time Alexander's agility put him in serious trouble. He did reach the fortress before Glaucias, but the Macedonians were being held at bay when Glaucias' troops arrived at the rear of Alexander's army. Alexander had failed to storm the fortress and was planning to lay siege to Pellion when Glaucias occupied the hill that would have served as retreat. Surrounded and outnumbered, the Macedonians seemed doomed by Alexander's impetuosity, but in the event that same quality saved the day.

Three types of helmets worn by Alexander's soldiers: RIGHT A Boetian helmet found in the river Tigris, possibly left by one of Alexander's soldiers. BELOW The simplest kind of Theban helmet. Smooth and conical, it was usually made of bronze strips riveted together. This one, however, was cast in one piece. BOTTOM RIGHT A Thracian helmet of the fifth century BC.

Greek sailing ships.
The Greeks designed their
galleys for speed and
manoeuvrability: long, with
narrow tapered hulls. The
trireme, a warship with three
banks of oarsmen, was both
faster and more compact than
the two-oared bireme (right).

Instead of trying to attack the enemy, he disconcerted them. The twelve thousand men in Alexander's command began with drill movements performed silently and at the double. Then at a signal, they all screamed 'Alalai' and beat their swords on their shields.

Quite unbelievably, the troops on the hillside fled to the fortress at Pellion. There was still the matter of trying to approach the fortress while the other troops held their ground. Alexander solved this problem, too, by having catapults mounted and used as field artillery covering the advance of the army. This first known use of catapults as field cover allowed the army to proceed without a casualty. Three days later Glaucias and Cleitus rested their armies together, thinking that the Macedonians had been routed. Alexander surprised them with a sudden attack, which left Illyria peaceful for the remainder of Alexander's reign.

News reached Greece that Alexander had been killed fighting the Triballians. Demosthenes, ever eager to capitalise on Alexander's misfortune, introduced a soldier to the Athenians who claimed to have seen Alexander fall. At the same time the Persians were not letting any chance pass to subvert peace in Greece. Darius' 'Golden Archers' (coins showing on one side the Great King as an archer) were hard at work bribing Greek statesmen against Macedonian suzerainty. Demosthenes helped supply Thebes with arms and wrote to Persian generals in Asia declaring it was time to fight Macedonia. Athens committed its support to Thebes and the Thebans appealed for help to neighbouring Arcadians, Argives and Eleans. The peace that Alexander had tried to impose on Greece with the threat of force was in shambles.

The Thebans took a vigorous initiative against Macedonia, but her allies were more generous with encouragement than actual help. The Macedonian garrison in Thebes became the focus of attack. The Thebans surrounded it with deep trenches and heavy stockades to prevent reinforcements or supplies getting in. The garrison commander tried to strengthen the walls and bring in a supply of missiles in preparation for a desperate defence.

At this point Alexander suddenly appeared after a prodigious forced march of over thirteen days. News that these were Alexander's troops was disbelieved, partly because of the reports of his death and partly because of the unheard-of feat of marching three hundred miles in two weeks. With thirty thousand infantry and three thousand cavalry Alexander was hoping that the size of his troops would convince the Thebans to sue for peace. The Macedonian force camped for three days outside the Electra Gates of the city, waiting for a Theban change of mind. Instead of wavering, though, the Thebans became more resolute in demanding their political freedom. A Macedonian herald shouted the message that any Thebans who wanted peace could join Alexander's troops and share the peace common to all of Greece. The Thebans shouted back that any Macedonian could join them in overthrowing the tyrant of Greece. Alexander is said to have been stunned by the audacity of the Thebans. He certainly proceeded vigorously to prepare the siege machines and strategy for subduing the city.

Thebes's allies did not rush to their aid now that they were in obvious danger. The Athenians voted to support the Thebans – but sent no troops. The Peloponnesian states did send troops, but they refused to cross the isthmus until they had a better idea of their chances against Alexander. Spiritual portents were no more encouraging. A large spider's web which spun itself in the Temple of Demeter was interpreted as a sign that the gods had deserted the Thebans. At the time of Alexander's arrival the statues in the Theban market place were purported to have burst out in a cold sweat and become bathed in moisture. City officials were told of the sound of a bellows coming from the marsh at Onchestus, while the waters of Dirce were covered with blood.

The Thebans were determined as ever. They built an outer wall to the city which the cavalry were assigned to defend. The enfranchised slaves and resident aliens defended the city walls while the main body of the Theban phalanx assembled outside the walls to confront the Macedonian phalanx. Alexander had divided his troops into three groups. The first attacked the new city wall, the second confronted the Theban phalanx and the third was held in reserve.

The fighting was intense. Spears and missiles were soon expended, so the two sides were locked in exhausting and slow sword battle. The Macedonians were more numerous and experienced, but the Thebans evenly matched them with determination. While the men fought to keep their city out of slavery, the women and children had fled to the temples

Recent excavations at the Electra Gates, Thebes.

where they offered unceasing sacrifices and implored the gods to save them.

Alexander called in his reserves, who were initially able to kill a large body of Thebans. But the Thebans gathered their courage and jeered that the Macedonians needed reinforcements. Alexander lost ground again once the Theban defence reestablished itself.

The change in fortunes was swift and terrible. The leader of a Macedonian phalanx battalion found an unguarded gate

to the city. He entered it and drew the Thebans into a stampede towards the walls to save their families and possessions. There was complete disorder with Thebans trampling each other as they rushed back inside. Undefended people were crowded in the narrow streets and indefensible civic areas of the city; they were at the mercy of their attackers. The Macedonian troops in the garrison now broke out of their confinement within the city and joined in the carnage. The Thebans fought on, begging no mercy. The Macedonians showed none, slaughtering and pillaging so that 'every corner of the city was piled high with corpses', in the words of the Greek historian Diodorus.

Alexander was said to have saved the life of one Theban woman who was brought to him because she had killed a

Troops close in on a fourth-century city. Within the walls, guards man the battlements; from the 'Monument of the Nereids' at Xanthus.

Macedonian general. She had told the general to look for her valuables in a well, into which she pushed him when he did. Though she was defiant even towards Alexander, the king admired her pluck and so she was spared along with a few priests, the family of the poet Pindar and some citizens who were recognised as friends of Macedonia. The rest, twenty thousand in all, were sold into slavery. Six thousand had been killed in battle and what was left of Thebes was razed. The decimation of the city was made the responsibility of the League of Corinth, since Alexander left the decision to them, though he knew the enemies of Thebes made its destruction a foregone conclusion.

The vengeance wreaked in Thebes, even if – as defenders of Alexander have contended – it was caused by the Macedonian

73

allies and not Alexander's troops themselves, destroyed any pretence of cooperation between the head of the League of Corinth and his Greek allies. Alexander could have what he wanted from the Greeks, but only by intimidation.

Athens was justifiably frightened by the news of Thebes's destruction. The celebration of the great mysteries of Demeter, an important Athenian event, was curtailed to give Athenians a chance to bring all their property within the city gates and await their fate. Alexander made it clear that he held some Athenians as guilty as the Thebans for the revolt. The Assembly voted to send a delegation of ten citizens who were known to be particularly favoured by Alexander to offer congratulations and assure him of the loyalty of the city.

74

A lion hunt frieze from the
sarcophagus found at Sidon.
Alexander is seen hunting
with Abdalonymus, later
king of Sidon.

Alexander replied that he wanted the surrender of eight Athenians, including Demosthenes and Lycurgus (the leader of the city), who were held to be accomplices of Thebes. The demand threw Athens into turmoil. Phocion, a highly respected Athenian general who perceived the futility of defying Alexander, recommended that the eight Athenians be surrendered. He said in the Assembly, 'If the king were to demand my close friend Nicocles, I should urge you to give him up. And if I were able to sacrifice myself to save you, I should consider that a happy fate. It is enough to have to mourn the loss of Thebes. It is better to ask for mercy and give in to the victors, both for you and for them, than to fight.'

Demosthenes argued that resistance was better than capitulation, for it was not only his own life that was at stake. He repeated the fable of the sheep who gave their watchdogs to the wolves and called Alexander the lone wolf of Macedonia. Those to be surrendered being the most esteemed citizens of Athens, Demosthenes had recourse to another analogy. 'Corn merchants sell consignments of their stock by showing some grains of wheat which they carry with them,' he said. 'In the same way, if you deliver us up, you are giving up yourselves, every one of you.'

The Athenians were loath to make a choice. They decided to try one more embassy to Alexander, this time headed by Demades, a friend of the king's who was paid five talents to undertake the mission. Begging Alexander a second time achieved what the king wanted; he was able to appear generous by dismissing his demand without fearing Athens's continued recalcitrance. Demosthenes had to retire in humiliation, and power devolved on the party of Demades and supporters of Alexander.

Other states were similarly quick to make amends for their support of Thebes. The Arcadians killed their anti-Macedonian leaders. The Eleans took back the pro-Macedonians who had been in exile. The Aetolians begged pardon from Alexander. Taking advantage of this situation, Alexander had the repentant states pledge their support for his invasion of Asia at a meeting of the League of Corinth. They agreed on the contingents that would be required and Alexander visited the Delphic oracle on his way back to Pella. He wanted some assurance of success for his imminent journey to Asia, but having arrived on an inauspicious day, the prophetess refused to officiate. Though she explained several times that by law she was forbidden to deliver a reply, Alexander urged her on to the temple. In exasperation she gave him the answer he wanted. He gave a donation of one hundred and fifty 'Philips', the gold slaters that had been minted by his father, and proceeded to Macedonia for the winter.

It was resolved that the expedition should begin the following spring, 334. His own generals, Parmenio and Antipater, urged Alexander to wait long enough to marry and have an heir before setting out on such a precarious mission. The wisdom of the advice was to be proved later, but for now the king showed only impatience at the suggestion. Whether out of inclination, the desire to get started, or fear for the treasury of Macedonia which was now dangerously depleted, Alexander was bent on starting the journey at the earliest opportunity.

4
Darius
of Persia

WHEN ALEXANDER SET OUT FOR ASIA in the spring of 334, he had little idea of the lengths to which his ambition would carry him. With an army that numbered about 35,000, no women and a small baggage train, he had the resources to support only a modest incursion on the Persian Empire. He had had to leave Macedonian forces of fifteen thousand infantry and fifteen hundred cavalry with Antipater, now the regent in Pella. During the winter preparations Alexander had even distributed royal property to pay for outfitting the army, so his resources were strained despite the booty taken from Thebes and Thrace. If not actually in debt, Alexander was still in dire need of funds to underwrite his venture.

Indeed, part of the reason for undertaking the crossing so quickly was to replenish the coffers of the treasury. Enemies would have to be sought where they did not present themselves, in order to exact the tribute needed to support the army. Besides, Alexander had always been generous with his troops and now no less than before he had to find booty to bolster their loyalty as they undertook an invasion with no set limits or familiar enemies. They went, at least, with justifiable confidence. Alexander had already proved his resourcefulness and bravery. He had been bold without being reckless. When he drove his troops hard on enforced marches, he had proved he could command with a decisiveness that had saved his men from many a critical situation. There was no obstacle that intimidated him. It was he who had established the reputation that was intimidating.

Many of what now seemed to be the king's precocious characteristics were to remain ingrained in him. His overwhelming drive to seek out further adventures and battles was manifest from the time he was sixteen and was never to leave him. Throughout the expedition he remained close to his mother. They corresponded and she was an important source of information about affairs in Macedonia. Alexander sent her much of the booty he acquired, especially luxuries from the Persian court. Nevertheless he never expressed an interest in returning to Macedonia. Court intrigues during the expedition allowed Alexander to remove Macedonian influences in his army and to squelch any voices that might counsel return. Respectful of all religions, Alexander sought out oracles and religious men along the way to advise him. There is no doubt that he was deeply superstitious,

PREVIOUS PAGES Detail of Darius enthroned from a large red-figure vase *c.* 325 BC, known as the Darius vase.

OPPOSITE Greek hoplites, heavily armed foot-soldiers, in combat against Persian cavalrymen.

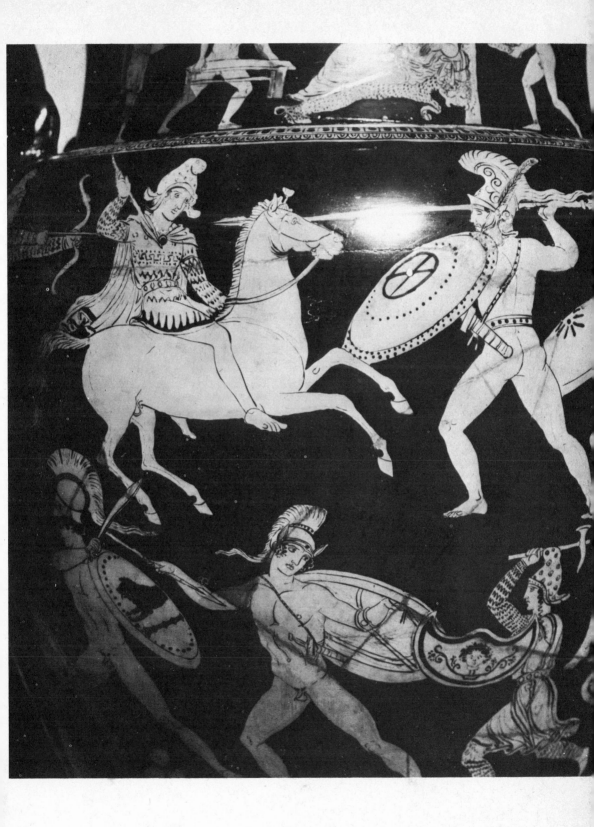

but rather than follow oracles, he seemed more intent on making them confirm what he had already decided to do. He usually got his way with gods because he had his way with men, but to his contemporaries there was every reason to assume that his favour came in fact from the gods. Alexander's sexual practices have been little discussed by historians. He was given a eunuch, whom he seems to have kept until the end of his life. He was also married and had a posthumously born son. Macedonian practice seems to have been as immoderate and undiscriminating in sex as in drink, with sex and drink as common accompaniments to celebrations. Plutarch takes pains to paint the picture of a saintly, abstemious king, but too many important events resulted from long drinking sessions to think that they occurred infrequently.

To temper the impetuousness in Alexander's nature, there was Parmenio on the expedition as second in command. He had led the advance party to Asia Minor that Philip had ordered two years before and he now held an entrenched position in the army. The troops on the journey included a cavalry of six squadrons which Parmenio commanded on the left of the phalanx. The cavalry of six squadrons on the right was under Alexander's command. Philotas, Parmenio's son, was at the head of the cavalry brigade. Coenus, a regimental commander, was a son-in-law of Parmenio's, possibly the new husband of Attalus' widow. And Nicanor, another of Parmenio's sons, led the infantry brigade. So the influence of the second in command had reason to cause some concern to Alexander. Cleitus, who was to save Alexander's life at the first battle of Asia Minor, commanded the exclusive cavalry guard.

The immediate goal of the journey was to liberate the Greek cities of Asia Minor from Persian rule. The Pan-Hellenic nature of the enterprise was emphasised by the inclusion of Thracian javelin throwers, one thousand Agrianians (whom Alexander particularly valued and kept close to him), fifteen hundred Thessalians and five hundred Cretan archers. The Macedonian troops, the core of the army, numbered twelve thousand infantry and eighteen hundred cavalry. The resolution to avenge Xerxes' conquest of the Greeks one hundred and fifty years before had been Philip's reason for marshalling troops for the expedition. It was adopted by Alexander, but avenging such an ancient grievance was as much an excuse now as it had been for Philip in his attempt to cajole support from the League of Corinth.

The Persians had been given enough warning to be waiting with a substantial army of their own. The twenty thousand Greek mercenaries (as opposed to Alexander's five thousand) were a unit larger than any single element in Alexander's army, but the two forces were, on the whole, of equal strength. Darius himself was not on hand for this first confrontation, which was led instead by Memnon of Rhodes, the most competent of the Persian leaders. The rest of the troops consisted of the satraps' personal forces. They were to have one supreme opportunity to beat Alexander back in this, their first encounter, but they were unable to put together a coordinated attack. Memnon provided wise advice, but it was ignored by the other Persian leaders. This missed opportunity was never to come again, for Alexander proceeded from strength to strength. His aggressive determination was able to pierce the shallow defences of an empire that was known to be poor in everything but money.

Darius III, the king of Persia against whom Alexander was marching, had attained his throne only two years earlier, in 336. Previously a member of the Persian court, he was elevated to the kingship by Bagoas, the satrap of upper Egypt. Bagoas had been the power behind the throne of the two previous Persian kings, the last of the Achaemenid line, whom Bagoas had murdered. 'A eunuch in physical fact but a militant rogue in disposition', as Diodorus the historian put it, Bagoas chose Darius to be king for his bravery: 'Among the Persians he was conceded first place in prowess.' Darius had been the only Persian to accept a challenge to single combat made by a Cadusian while the Persian army was fighting a campaign against that northern tribe. When Darius killed the enemy, he was honoured by King Artaxerxes III, the first king Bagoas had poisoned. Bagoas tried to have Darius murdered after putting him on the throne, but with poetic justice Darius made his benefactor drink the poison that had been prepared for him.

Such machinations were the product of a nation in the throes of a long decline, a condition of much benefit to Alexander. Xerxes' invasion in 480 BC had been the last of Persia's direct threats to Greek states. Though the Persians were soundly defeated in the naval battle of Salamis in

A vase in the form of a
trireme. Hellenistic from
Vulci. The pointed prow
acted as a battering ram.

480 BC, the weakness of the empire was obscured by the
Greeks' inability to end their own conflict and combine
against the Persians. In fact, Darius II was able to capitalise
on Greek conflict and in 387 conclude the King's Peace
which gave him a nominal hegemony over Greece. The
interference of Persians in Greek affairs was primarily
through bribery, the king being well supplied with bullion
and his gold 'archers'.

But for any kind of action he was dependent on satraps
who in some cases had resources and power denied the king.
The whole of the empire was divided into twenty satrapies,
which were so independent that satraps had the right to
coin money and raise troops. The Achaemenids had
provided Persia with two centuries of relative peace, but not
because of their strength. They had merely overseen a system
that was so diffuse and decentralised that isolated revolts

and troublesome tribes never caused universal upheaval. The king himself even paid tribute to tribes guarding mountain passes that lay between his several capitals. Towards such insubordination Alexander was to show ruthless scorn, though he too was made to understand the expediency of cooperating with elements of an empire that could be contained but in no way governed centrally.

There was also a docility in eastern peoples which took Alexander some getting used to after the fierce independence of Greek states. A new notion of kingship was to be discovered in the Persian Empire. As Macedonian king, he was first among the equals at court. In Persia the king was an entity distinct even from his possessions, creating an anomalous situation in which the title of king could be – and was after Alexander's death – inherited independently of any territories to which it might have originally referred. Only in this society could the cult of Alexander's divinity thrive. The Asian practice of subjects prostrating themselves before the king was ridiculed by Alexander's Companions when they were introduced to it, but it was the common practice among the orientals.

Alexander was not just being opportunistic and using an Asian custom to promote his own glory. In an era of many gods and diverse religious cults even within one society, his tolerance and undifferentiated respect were understandable as well as useful. He was welcomed by many a city for overthrowing the despotic conquests of the Persians, who often destroyed native temples to assure the docility of the peoples.

The Asian expedition got under way in May 334. In only three weeks Alexander had marched his troops from Pella to the embarkation port on the Hellespont. Parmenio arranged the crossing in 160 triremes, the galleys with three banks of oars. Alexander went ahead to begin his venture with religious celebration and entreaties to the gods to endow the journey with success.

The sacrifice of a bull was performed on the ship travelling across the Hellespont to propitiate Poseidon. Libations were poured into the sea for the Nereids. At the shore, Alexander supposedly planted a spear as a declaration of his intention to conquer all of Asia. This disputed event has been argued as proof of the full extent of Alexander's

Destruction of Troy, from an Attic vase. By the time of Alexander's visit, Troy had long decayed to the status of a village. The citizens supposed that Alexander would like to see the lyre of his namesake, better known as Paris of Troy. However, Achilles was the hero with whom Alexander identified.

ambition, but such a gesture, even if it did occur, did not specifically entail a set course of action. Anxious to get to the site of Troy, Alexander offered sacrifices to Zeus on shore and moved quickly towards the city of his hero and ancestor, Achilles.

In Troy, Alexander sacrificed to Athena and made a gift of his armour to her temple, taking in return some weapons said to have been from the Trojan War. He paid homage to the grave of Achilles, anointing the column marking its

place with oil. He then ran a race naked in front of the grave
with his Companions – according to the custom – and crowned
it with a wreath. He is said to have remarked how lucky
Achilles was to have a Homer to sing the praises of his
exploits after his death.

For Alexander had taken the natural step of bringing a
historian with him, but one who hardly matched the stature
of Homer. Callisthenes, nephew of Aristotle, was more a
publicist than a reputable historian. Aristotle himself said

that he had the gifts of speech but lacked wisdom, yet he still might have been able to write an account of Alexander's journey to garner support from the Greeks, as he was supposed to do. Unfortunately, Callisthenes alienated his patron and the Macedonian army. Though his account of the journey is lost, fragments do exist and it was available to other Alexander chroniclers, including Plutarch. We know that he exaggerated Alexander's exploits. Here, in the beginning of the expedition, he emphasised Alexander's similarities to Achilles, as related in Homer's account in the *Iliad*. Later, he cited Alexander as a god, a point that suited his role as flatterer (but it may also have reflected the way Alexander wanted himself to be presented). It is reported that Callisthenes knew his *Exploits of Alexander* was an inferior work to a previous history of Greece, *Hellenica*, for he admitted the discrepancy by saying, 'I wrote the better one when I was hungry and this one when I was well fed.' So Alexander had good reason to regret the lack of a Homer since it is on this historian of admitted failings that all subsequent biographies have had to depend – to the extent that Callisthenes' account was available.

The rest of Alexander's personal staff consisted of body-guards and Companions. The former, numbering no more than eight, were probably chosen for personal rather than military reasons. Hephaestion, Alexander's lifelong friend, was probably one of these. In Troy, when Alexander laid the wreath on Achilles' tomb, Hephaestion laid one on Patroclus', showing that the closeness of these two men paralleled the closeness of their forebears, as described by Homer. The Companions comprised a larger group of up to a hundred, who acted as a king's council. From this group were to come the governors and administrators of the empire.

Having paid his respects at Troy, Alexander had little time to await his first confrontation with the Persians. He met his troops where they camped after landing and together they proceeded eastward towards the river Granicus (now called the Koçabas). There the Persian forces were waiting. The river, though not large, was swollen with spring rains. Across the water, forty thousand Persians were massed, cavalry in front and Greek mercenary infantry behind. Memnon had cautioned his fellow Persians to retreat and await Darius before confronting Alexander.

OPPOSITE Achilles binding Patroclus' wound. It is evident by the tribute paid to the tombs that Alexander and Hephaestion identified strongly with their Greek forebears.

Alexander's Official Sculptor

Lysippus, who was invited to serve the
court at Pella, specialised in the execution
of bronze statues, which he produced at
a prodigious rate. He is said to have made
fifteen hundred statues, the most famous of
which were of Alexander. The first so
delighted the young Macedon that Lysippus
was granted the sole right to sculpt his
likeness. Lysippus depicted Alexander as a
great military genius and statesman of
exceptional but human gifts; his depiction of
the physical nature of man makes him the
founder of realistic portraiture.

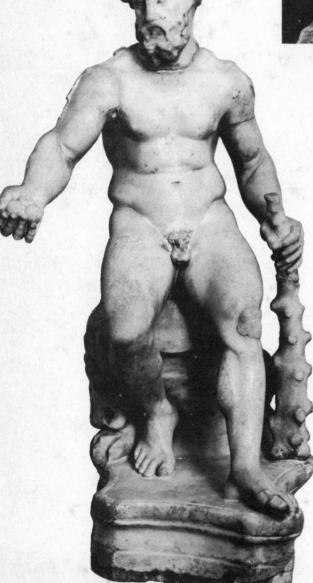

ABOVE The Azara Herm, a bust of
Alexander thought to be after Lysippus.
LEFT Lysippus made a number of statues
of Heracles in different situations and
moods, the most famous of which
shows him in middle age, his Labours
completed.
RIGHT 'Apoxyomenos' or 'Athlete scraping
himself clean'.

But they were impatient and insulted at the suggestion that they couldn't dispatch the enemy themselves. They had chosen a superior position on the east bank of the Granicus from which they had every expectation of repelling Alexander with unceremonious haste.

Parmenio even advised Alexander to postpone crossing the river until the next day. Alexander refused, saying with characteristic bravado, 'It would be shameful if a trickle of water like this stopped us when we crossed the Hellespont with no trouble.' There was also the strategic advantage to Alexander of showing no hesitancy but meeting the enemy as quickly and forthrightly as possible.

The Persians were waiting on the other side, gathered at the top of the steep river bank. The cavalry stood in front of the infantry, not for a strategic advantage, but merely to hold the honoured position of attack. In fact, with the muddy bank separating the forces, the cavalry would have done better to fall in behind the infantry. Instead, the cavalry stood its ground and showered the Macedonians with javelins as they reached the shore. Alexander's forces suffered heavy casualties at first, but the Persians, being immobilised at the top of the bank, were soon engaged in hand-to-hand fighting with the advancing Macedonians – 'a cavalry battle but on infantry lines', as the historian Arrian described the close-range encounter.

Alexander himself was soon in the thick of battle. Noticeable for his white-plumed helmet and personal following, he attracted attack from the leading Persian commanders. They put all of their effort into killing Alexander; so the rest of the Macedonian forces had a much easier time of crossing. Alexander fought the onslaught 'horse pressed against horse, man against man, wrestling with one another . . .' as Arrian says. The personal danger to Alexander was severe. In the face of the concerted Persian attack Alexander broke his spear. He asked his groom for another, but his had broken too. In this emergency a personal bodyguard supplied his to Alexander, who then immediately began chasing Darius' son-in-law Mithridates. Though Alexander was able to strike Mithridates in the face and hurl him to the ground, other Persian commanders soon reinforced the attack and held Alexander at bay. Rhoesakes rode at Alexander brandishing a scimitar, its curved blade coming down with full impact on Alexander's helmet. Plutarch

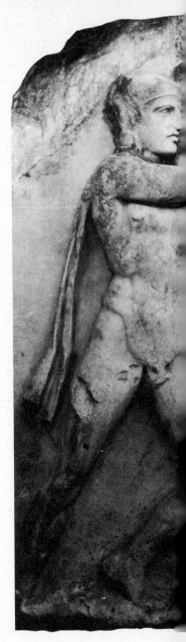

ABOVE Greeks fighting Orientals, from the Nereid Monument, Xanthus.

OVERLEAF Detail from the 'Alexander Sarcophagus'.
This side depicts Alexander attacking a Persian
horseman at Issus.

reports that Alexander's hair was grazed by the blow. Certainly the helmet was destroyed, but Alexander managed to strike him through the breastplate with his spear and Rhoesakes fell. Spithridates, another Persian commander, came up on horseback behind Alexander. He rose up in the stirrups to whack Alexander in the head with a battle axe. Just then, Cleitus, the cavalry guard leader, chopped off Spithridates' arm with his sword. Three of the Persian leaders had fallen without killing Alexander.

The Persian effort had failed to kill Alexander and now their whole army was at the mercy of the Macedonian troops. The Persian forces turned and fled, but the Greek mercenaries in the Persian rearguard held their ground. They soon asked for mercy, which Alexander denied them – an impetuous move which cost the lives of many of his infantry. Perhaps he wanted to make an example of these traitors to the Greek cause; perhaps it was just a rash decision made in the heat of battle. There were many Macedonian casualties, but they managed to slaughter the mercenaries. Two thousand were taken prisoner and sent back to hard labour in Macedonia. Strategically, such ruthlessness was counterproductive, for it only strengthened the resistance of beaten troops; Alexander wisely changed his policy soon thereafter.

The figure of ninety given as the number of Alexander's troops killed is suspiciously low. There were at least twenty-five Companions killed in the first assault, for Alexander had Lysippus, his chosen sculptor, make statues of these men in bronze. The families of the other dead were granted immunity from taxes and excused of all debt in property and service. As an offering to Athena, Alexander sent three hundred shields to Athens, inscribed: 'Alexander, son of Philip, and all the Greeks, except Sparta, won these spoils of war from the barbarians who dwell in Asia.' Notably absent is any mention of Macedonians, the main fighting unit. The explicit exclusion of Sparta makes a pointed reminder of their refusal to join the League of Corinth. Most of the rest of the plunder, from purple hangings to drinking vessels, Alexander sent to his mother.

The fruits of the victory came immediately. The cities which resisted paying homage to Alexander upon his arrival in Asia Minor lost no time in doing so now. Alexander had had to bypass Zeleia, a Greek city that lay on the way to

Granicus, but it now surrendered. Having been the chief Persian base, it could blame its tardiness on the coercion of the Persians. And so Alexander excused their collaboration with the enemy. Other Greek cities in Asia Minor also surrendered themselves. One of them, Lampsacus, Alexander was contemplating destroying because of its defection after Parmenio had freed it two years before. But bowing to the entreaties of its leading citizen, Alexander spared the city, while not changing it in any way that would indicate that it was 'freer' than it had been under the Persians.

Only when he got to Ephesus did Alexander hit upon a policy by which the Greek Asia Minor cities could be considered liberated. Ephesus itself had been ruled by an oligarchy sympathetic to the Persians. While replacing the oligarchy with a democracy, Alexander prevented the new government from taking vengeance on their previous leaders. More important, during his stay in Ephesus representatives from other Asia Minor cities made appeals to Alexander to visit them, since they had expelled their Persian garrisons and established democracies for themselves. As a result, Alexander sent Parmenio with a squadron of cavalry and five thousand infantry to take over the cities. They were confirmed as democracies, given back to their own rule of law and remitted their tribute to the Persians. The situation was of course made advantageous to the cities as a means of placating them and assuring their loyalty. Alexander's motives beyond that – any form of political idealism – have to be discounted. After all, his own relationship with Greek democracies, notably Athens, could not have left a favourable impression on the young king.

Before leaving Ephesus, Alexander offered to rebuild the temple that had burned down at his birth. The proud Ephesians, showing the limit of their gratitude to Alexander, refused. In turn, Alexander would not remit the tribute to the city outright, but he did have it given for rebuilding the temple. At his next stop, however, in the small city of Priene, Alexander was allowed to dedicate the Temple of Athena after contributing handsomely to its restoration.

The only two Asia Minor cities that now resisted Alexander's advance were the ports of Miletus and Halicarnassus. Both of them were capable of being defended by the Persian fleet. Alexander was particularly anxious to

A silver coin of Ephesus showing a bee (with *epsilon* and *phi*, the first two letters of Ephesus in Greek, on either side of it) and, on the reverse, a stag beside a palm tree. The bee and stag were both symbols in the cult of Artemis, whose temple, destroyed at the time of Alexander's birth, he had rebuilt.

OPPOSITE A statue of Alexander from Priene.

take them and deny access to the Persians' four hundred ships. Miletus had already surrendered to Alexander, but at news of the approach of the Persian fleet, retracted its surrender. Unfortunately for the Miletians, the Greek fleet with only one hundred and sixty ships was even closer and so was able to blockade the port. Persian ships were forced to go ten miles to the Meander river for water and then even farther to the island of Samos for supplies. Alexander's troops had little trouble breaking through Miletus' outer wall. The city was taken with the help of fire-brandishing siege machines, and its three hundred last defenders swam out to an islet in the harbour, fearing Alexander's ruthless policy towards mercenaries. It was here that he changed his tactics and promised no punishment to those mercenaries who joined his forces, a gesture that was to save many lives during Alexander's subsequent career.

Alexander deliberately chose to avoid a naval encounter despite Parmenio's counsel to mount an attack by sea. Parmenio believed that the Greek fleet could beat the Persians and that even a Macedonian defeat would be no worse than *not* fighting. Besides, he had seen a favourable omen. Watching an eagle on the bank near the Greek fleet, he took it as a sign of sure victory, for which he was willing to risk his own life by joining the fleet himself. Alexander disputed both the strategic and oracular advice of Parmenio,

ABOVE Lion from the Mausoleum at Halicarnassus.
RIGHT A carved stone lion from the Temple of Apollo at Didyma,
eleven miles from Miletus. The renowned oracle of Apollo had been
mute for over a century; the temple lay in ruins. On Alexander's arrival
the oracle was heard to speak again – uttering his name. Possibly as
a result of the flattering predictions the temple was rebuilt.

saying that he had no intention of sacrificing his men as a gesture to experienced Phoenician and Cypriot sailors. As for the omen, the eagle appeared over land and to Alexander that meant the victory of Alexander's *army* over the Persian navy.

At this juncture Alexander's uneasiness about his fleet induced him to disband it and send the ships back to Greece. Twenty Athenian ships were kept, but probably as no more then hostages for Athens's good behaviour. Disbanding the fleet was a rash decision since their help against Miletus had been indispensable. Financial stringency has been

blamed for an otherwise mysterious move, but Alexander was more probably concerned most about the loyalty of the largely Athenian fleet. Early the next year he had enough money to recruit another fleet, so he could have kept this one had he wanted to.

Alexander's next venture, the siege of the Carian capital – Halicarnassus – had to be undertaken without benefit of the fleet. A division of the Persian fleet lay in the harbour and the city's defence was organised by Memnon, the best of Darius' generals. It had three fortresses, a high brick wall and a 23-foot deep moat which was 45 feet wide. Inside, Memnon commanded two thousand mercenaries and a large body of Asian soldiers. These defenders successfully countered Alexander's attempt to fill in the moat and implant the siege machines close to the wall. A surprise attack on Alexander's encampment forced the attackers themselves to move round to another side of the city. A new brick wall was hastily built to cover the first breach that Alexander's forces put in the city's defences.

Gradually the Macedonians wore down the defenders. Sorties against Alexander's siege machines took a heavy toll on the defences. The wall was destroyed in some places, damaged in others. Memnon decided on one last major attack against the Macedonians. But the Macedonian troops outside the wall were too much for the Persians. As they tried to retreat back into the city, the gates were closed too soon, lest some Macedonians get in. Those Persians left outside were slaughtered.

As a last resort, Memnon decided himself to set fire to the city and the inhabitants had to retreat to strongholds on high ground and a harbour island. Buildings by the outer wall were put to the torch. The wind quickly spread the flames. Alexander ordered up all his troops – though it was now near midnight – to try to save the town. Those found setting fires were slaughtered on the spot, while the Macedonian encampment became a refuge open to the city's inhabitants. By morning the Persian troops had installed themselves in the two strongholds, which they were to occupy for another twelve months. Alexander left them there, knowing that they had little chance of beating the three thousand mercenaries he left with their commander Ptolemy as a garrison in the town.

Alexander was able to take advantage of internecine fighting that had been going on among the royalty of Caria. This small

106

kingdom in the south-east corner of Asia Minor now had as its ruler the brother of the slain king Pixodarus. Pixodarus' widow had retreated to a fortress which she surrendered peaceably to Alexander. This was a base to start the next year's campaign. For the moment, he called her queen of Caria and she made him her son with the legitimate rights of an heir.

For the main body of Alexander's troops this was the conclusion to a successful year's campaign. With no women travelling with the army, the soldiers were understandably elated by the home leave Alexander gave to the troops who had been married just before the campaign. 'No act of Alexander's ever made him more loved by his troops,' relates Arrian. Officers were sent with the men to recruit more soldiers for the next year's campaign. Parmenio took the siege machines, baggage wagons and the major contingent of soldiers back to Sardis in central Asia Minor with orders to meet Alexander later in the year in Gordium.

Alexander himself led a small group of soldiers to take the rest of the southern Asia Minor coast in an attempt to set the Persian fleet adrift. He would do his best to 'conquer the Persian fleet on land' as he had been forced to say when confronted with the weakness of his own navy. The rough terrain made a large body of troops impractical and, as it turned out, unnecessary.

During this winter campaign, according to Arrian, Alexander had been subject to an ominous event which came to characterise the whole of the undertaking. During a nap, Alexander had been annoyed by a swallow twittering loudly round his head 'in a way that seemed to express unusual alarm'. Aristander of Telmessus, the seer who had foretold the miraculous birth of Alexander himself, said it portended a friend's treachery. Sure enough, Parmenio sent word that a captured envoy from Darius had revealed a plot on Alexander's life. The envoy was going to convey to Alexander of Lyncestis an offer of a thousand talents in gold and the Macedonian crown for killing Alexander.

Alexander consulted with his Companions who advised killing their accused fellow officer without delay. He had been, they recalled, brother to the men who killed Alexander's father. But because of sympathy for Antipater (this Alexander's father-in-law) or for some other reason, Alexander again saved his life, as he had done at the time of the regicide.

Ancient Gordium. 'There were thunderclaps and flashes of lightning that very night', conveniently signifying Zeus' approval. So Alexander offered sacrifice to the 'gods who had sent signs and ratified his loosing of the knot'.

Other distractions occurred, like the need to go to Aspendus a second time when the town reneged on their promise to pay a tribute of fifty talents. It was a particularly large amount for a small state to pay, leading some scholars to speculate that Alexander was now short of funds. Because of their unwillingness to comply with the fifty-talent levy, Alexander raised the amount to a hundred talents and took the leading citizens as hostages. But, to add another meaning to the twittering sparrow's visit, Alexander had been able to conquer the greater part of Asia Minor with opposition that amounted to little more than annoyance.

Here on the threshold of Asia, only months away from the encounter with the Great King of Persia which was to change the balance of power in the known world, Alexander was inspecting the symbol of mastery over Asia. The Gordian knot, by tradition capable of being untied by the man who would rule Asia, was used to attach King Midas' wagon to the yoke used for pulling it. The wagon itself had been honoured in the acropolis of Gordium because it brought Midas to be king as had been foretold in a prophesy. The intricacy of the Gordian knot, its ends hidden in an interwoven pattern, required perhaps the patience and skill of a king to unravel. Alexander demonstrated his other regal attribute, audacity, by cutting the knot with his sword. No one questioned that he had accomplished the feat. If necessary, the gods would have to take their own revenge, for men provided too little resistance.

5 The Battle of Issus

THOUGH ALEXANDER had fought his way through Asia Minor, the Persians had not yet really committed themselves to the defeat of the Macedonian army. At the Granicus, Darius had not bothered to go himself or send enough troops to thrash Alexander. He had let Alexander do his marauding in Asia Minor with harassment only from the Persian fleet. He was in fact pleased to note Alexander's progress once he got into Asia Minor, for he assumed that the farther east the Macedonian army went, the easier it could be cut off from supplies and support in Greece. The Persian strategy followed the plans of the brilliant Persian general Memnon, who was relying on the Persian fleet moving westward to recapture areas as Alexander abandoned them.

Darius stayed safely tucked away in Asia while Alexander fought his way area by area among local rulers and armies. It is tempting but wrong to look on Alexander as David fighting the Persian king's Goliath, since Persian troops outnumbered the Macedonians only at the climactic battle of Gaugamela. Still, Darius had seemingly endless reserves to draw on. The Greek army had always maintained a high reputation in Asia and proved itself over and over against Persian troops. But Darius had been able to recruit substantial numbers of Greek mercenaries for himself, as well as having command of twenty independent satraps' armies. These resources were marshalled only gradually as Darius thought he needed them, a prudent policy but one which worked to Alexander's advantage.

Only in the spring of 333, when Alexander had marched through Asia Minor and cut the Gordian knot, did Darius decide to lead the Persian forces against the invader. Until now he might reasonably have assumed that there was no need to search out Alexander, for Memnon's naval counterattack was having spectacular success – to the extent that Alexander urgently sent five hundred talents specifically to acquire a new Greek fleet and six hundred talents more for Antipater to use against the Persians in Greece. Memnon had taken Chios and was fighting in Lesbos, the last island outposts of Asia Minor on the way to Greece itself. The eastern Aegean had once again become a Persian lake, much to the distress of Alexander, who at the moment had no fleet himself.

Just then, Memnon was killed in a battle on the island of Lesbos. Two of his subordinates took over the Persian offensive, but they lacked Memnon's capability and experience. In

PREVIOUS PAGES Alexander and Darius amidst the frenzy and fury at the battle of Issus. A mosaic, composed of minute stone and glass tesserae, it is the largest and most ambitious pictorial composition that has come down to us from antiquity.

terms of the overall Asian expedition, this has been considered Alexander's greatest stroke of luck. It required an immediate change in Persian strategy; Darius now decided to meet Alexander head-on.

Such a decision was not taken lightly or effortlessly by the Great King of Persia. His entourage and soldiers resembled a city on the march. Estimates of his mobile group varied from four-hundred thousand – the size of a substantial town – to well over half a million. Unlike Alexander's army, the baggage train and entourage were not kept to a minimum. There were palace staff, hordes of treasure, and even Darius' family. Alexander was to be awed at the booty left him after the battle.

Still, Darius was able to mobilise his army and get it up to Syria in the spring and summer of 333. During the summer he gradually grew impatient waiting for Alexander, who seemed to be dawdling at the corner of Asia before heading down the eastern coast of the Mediterranean. Darius had even assured Alexander's army passage through two severe straits – the Cilician and Syrian gates. These obstacles could have taken months to surmount, since a loaded camel could not get through the pass at the Cilician gates. In the strategy devised by Memnon, Alexander was to have free passage through the gates, so that he would get farther east, where he could be cut off and attacked more easily.

Alexander was delayed for other reasons. Between the Cilician and Syrian gates, he came down with a serious illness. Possibly already ill, Alexander had plunged into the icy waters of a mountain river during the exertions of the army's march. His doctors would not try any potent medicines for fear of being accused of regicide if they failed. Only Alexander's close personal friend and physician, Philip of Acarnania, would prepare a drastic potion capable of fighting the fever. During this illness, Parmenio wrote to Alexander warning him of another plot against the king's life. This time Parmenio named Philip of Acarnania as the conspirator whom Darius had paid to kill him. As Alexander lay ill and was approached by Philip with the potion, he handed him Parmenio's letter while he drank the draught. Though Philip was taken aback by the accusation against him, he was immediately reassured by Alexander's confidence. It was soon clear that the medicine was an effective purgative and Alexander began the long-awaited recovery. Alexander's lack of suspicion was an important sign of his regal confidence, a reminder of Aristotle's lessons in distinguishing the self-assured king from the eternally suspicious tyrant. Four years later, when Philotas was accused of plotting against the king, the story would unfortunately be different.

Not knowing the resolution of Alexander, Darius might well have construed necessary delay as a fear to fight the Great King of Persia. Though Alexander had never shown a reluctance to proceed with his expedition, the circumstances of his position might have cautioned delay. Halicarnassus and Miletus, places for which Alexander had fought hard, were lost. Agis III, the king of Sparta who had refused to join the League of Corinth, had begun his counterattack. He sent an envoy to Darius to plan a coordinated attack against Alexander, similar to the alliance that had given Persia hegemony in Greece after the King's Peace fifty years before. In his confidence while awaiting Alexander, Darius put off negotiations with Agis, but he certainly foresaw the quick demise of a Macedonian force that had obviously overextended itself.

In this frame of mind, Darius wanted to make sure that Alexander did not escape his clutches. Now that he had the Macedonians in Asia, he wanted to dispatch them and destroy once and for all their irksome meddling in Asian and Greek affairs. Darius also had the advice of flatterers in his entourage who wanted him to believe that Alexander was afraid of the impending confrontation.

Such advice encouraged Darius to think of chasing Alexander if Alexander was not coming as far as the plains of Syria. A defector from the Macedonian army strongly advised Darius to stay where he was. Alexander was no coward and the open plains gave every advantage to the large army of Persia, especially with its strong contingent of cavalry. Meantime, Alexander was further delayed by his celebrations and competitions after exacting two hundred talents in tribute from the Soli tribe. Darius' flatterers were by now saying that the presence of Darius himself had further weakened the resolve of the Macedonians, so that if Alexander were to be beaten, he would first have to be found. So Darius let himself be convinced that he had to chase Alexander. The mighty Persian army started moving north.

Each side had intelligence reports of the whereabouts of the other. They knew that both were along the eastern Mediterranean coast only hundreds of miles from each other and

OPPOSITE Alexander approached the Cilician Gates, ready for a confrontation. Surprisingly he was able to pass through the defile unopposed.

114

Alexander entered Tarsus
on 3 September 333 after a
rapid forced march from the
foothills of the Taurus.

heading for a confrontation north of Damascus. When Darius reached Damascus, he left most of his belongings and train in the city as he and the army headed north. As he moved south, Alexander left a field station of wounded men by the gulf of Issus, in the corner where the northern and eastern Mediterranean coasts meet. The two armies, as Plutarch put it, passed each other in the night. They went through different passes of the same mountains, leaving Alexander south of Darius. The Persian troops fell upon the Macedonian field station and killed all the soldiers they found there. The missed confrontation infuriated both sides. Though Alexander was in a better strategic position now that the Persians were hemmed in on the mountain passes, he deeply regretted the loss of his men. He sent a contingent of Companions back to check positively that Darius had made his way past the Macedonians. A galley of Macedonians was fitted out, since the Issus coast lay open to the Mediterranean, and the Companions confirmed the news to Alexander. Darius was elated to have fallen on the defenceless soldiers, but also disturbed that his intelligence had allowed him to miss Alexander. It was the Macedonians who immediately doubled back to catch the Persian army with its back to the sea.

The arduous march had left the Macedonians exhausted but Alexander could not let them relent, lest the Persians escape from this cul-de-sac. A contingent was immediately posted by the pass through which the Macedonians had gone down the coast. The rest of the army was kept on alert, but allowed to rest overnight, knowing that the Persians were no more than eight miles away. Darius realised that he was being cornered, but instead of trying to get out, he had all of his troops take positions close to the shore, backing against the sea. The next morning the Macedonian troops began a slow, methodical march towards the Persians. Parmenio, leading the left side of cavalry, was instructed to be sure to keep his extreme end rooted to the shore line, thus preventing any possible escape. The rest of the troops fanned out over the terrain as they approached the awaiting Persian troops.

By the time the Macedonians were within fighting distance it was late afternoon. Alexander had already mapped out his strategy so that the approach need not stop. For this confrontation with the army of the Great King of Persia, Alexander had exhorted his troops to take courage:

117

Our enemies are Medes and Persians, men who for centuries have lived soft and luxurious lives. We of Macedonia have been trained in the hard school of war and vigilance. Above all, we are free and they are slaves. There may be Greek troops in Persian service, but how different is their cause from ours! And finally you have Alexander: they – Darius.

Having assured the defensive role of Parmenio's left flank, Alexander strengthened the right wing, which was under his command. He secretly took two squadrons of mounted Companions from the centre and brought them to the right wing. When the deliberative, slow advance of the Macedonians suddenly got close to the Persians, Alexander ordered the charge. Leading his men across the river, he broke through immediately and caused the Persian left side to collapse. The Greek mercenaries in the Persian centre were able, however, to take advantage of the break between the Macedonian right and the centre, which lagged behind. Into this breach they poured and took a heavy toll of the Macedonian centre. The fighting here was furious and inconclusive.

Darius, meanwhile, standing in the centre of his line, was thrown back by the force of Alexander's attack coming from the right. Though the battle was in no way decided, the Great King suddenly turned and fled. His personal flight changed everything. Fighting continued with the same intensity, but the Persians had only their lives to save. Their 'cause' was fleeing in his chariot. When that proved too slow, he slipped off his armour, unhitched the chariot and jumped on one of the horses. Alexander pursued Darius until nightfall, but the chase was fruitless and the victors returned to the battlefield.

It was now that Alexander viewed Darius' possessions with awe. Even when he had come to fight, the king had been surrounded by the splendour of a magnificent court, from fragrant spices to the golden bowls and attendants to serve him. Alexander was appalled at the ostentation of it all, though he himself eventually succumbed to the style of the Persian court.

Darius was not only a fugitive. He had also lost a vast fighting machine. Of the twenty thousand mercenaries he had employed, he was left with two thousand who fled with him. Eight thousand fled in a body and found their way into the service of King Agis of Sparta. The Persian naval battle against Greece now collapsed, for Memnon's two successors had already proved to be ineffectual.

The Macedonians marched from Issus to the great commercial port of Sidon. Sidon welcomed Alexander, possibly hoping he would join forces against their neighbour and rival, Tyre.

The booty taken from the Persians included three thousand talents of gold that Darius was carrying with him, along with all the servants and attendants in his personal escort. There was also the royal family, consisting of Darius' wife, mother and two daughters. According to Plutarch, Alexander treated them with every mark of respect. Having heard that Darius' chariot and armour had been captured, they assumed he must be dead. Alexander, greatly affected by their distress, sent word to them that Darius had not been killed and they would continue to have 'everything they had been entitled to when Darius was king'. Alexander also let them bury the dead and take from the plunder the ornaments and clothes that they wanted. Though the queen was reputedly one of the most beautiful women in Asia, 'Alexander, so it seems, [according to Plutarch] thought it more worthy of a king to conquer his own emotions than an enemy and so he never went near these women.' His respect for them was such that when the queen mother later asked Alexander to save the Uxians, a tribe

120

demanding tribute at one Asian mountain pass, he did so.

An even larger amount of booty remained in Damascus. Alexander dispatched Parmenio and the Thessalians to fetch it. The choice of the Thessalians was made because of their magnificent performance during the battle of Issus. The booty they could plunder and keep made a handsome reward.

Alexander now had to decide whether to pursue Darius through Asia or continue his journey down the Mediterranean coast. Left with only a small body of troops, Darius would be easy prey for the Macedonian army once he was found, but the chase might be long and difficult. Killing Darius would automatically end any allegiance given him, so that the empire of Asia would be Alexander's. There was, however, the countervailing worry of a Greek uprising, an event that did not wholly depend on the support of Darius. In fact, Agis of Sparta had benefited from the rout of the Persian army by acquiring eight thousand more mercenaries to mount his attack on Macedonia. So Alexander decided not to abandon his communications with Greece, which pursuing Darius would entail. In his speech to his men, according to Arrian, Alexander explained his concern: 'To pursue Darius with the neutral city of Tyre in our rear and Egypt and Cyprus still in enemy hands would be a serious risk, especially in view of the situation in Greece.'

So the Macedonian army proceeded unmolested halfway down the coast towards Egypt, until it reached Tyre, a small island just off the coast of what is now southern Lebanon. Alexander could have passed here too unmolested, but his determination to subdue the Persian navy and secure the whole coast made him challenge the Tyrians despite their seemingly impregnable fortress. The old city of Tyre on the coast had been abandoned and all the citizens moved behind the walls of the 'new city' on an island half a mile from the shore. A Phoenician city-state renowned for its trading, Tyre was rich and well protected. Its long history is recalled in the Bible, the prophet Ezekiel being instructed by the Lord to say to the king of Tyre:

> Who was there like Tyre, fortified
> In the midst of the sea?
> When thy wares came forth out of the seas,
> Thou didst fill many peoples;
> With the multitude of thy riches and of thy merchandise
> Didst thou enrich the kings of the earth.

Such a wealthy, defensible city had no reason to accede to Alexander's request to be allowed to sacrifice at their Temple of Heracles. The Tyrian representatives said Alexander could use the temple on the shore, but they had no intention of letting a delegation within the walls of the island fortress. According to one source, there was also a tradition of letting only the king of Tyre sacrifice at this temple. Though the Tyrians could insist that they harboured no hostility towards Alexander, he was not prepared to accept their limited obeisance. The wisdom of his obstinacy has been questioned, especially in light of the tremendous resources needed for the attack. According to Diodorus, 'The Tyrians cheerfully faced the prospect of a siege', which then began in January 332.

Alexander began by ordering a 200-foot-wide causeway to be built to the island. Despite the distance, rapid progress was made when thousands of natives were pressed into service, using the walls and buildings of Old Tyre to reach the new city. At first the Tyrians mocked Alexander's audacious encroachment on the sea god's territory. Surely Poseidon would have his revenge. But the Tyrians nonetheless took the precaution of evacuating women and children to Carthage, the powerful north African city which was a colony of Tyre. Alexander's progress being greater than Tyre had expected, only a small number of the people were in fact evacuated before Alexander had reached close to the city walls. The native force of eighty triremes stopped ferrying people to Carthage and started to attack Alexander. The boats were manned with archers and slingers as well as offensive machinery. The Tyrians used stone-throwing machines mounted on light and heavy catapults which they rowed close to the builders of the causeway. Alexander retaliated by manning a ship himself and riding furiously with the small Greek navy towards the Tyrian harbour in the hope of cutting the attackers off from their port. The effort failed, but it did force the Tyrian ships to rush back to their port themselves.

Then, as now, warfare was a spur to technology. At that time, siege machines were capable of flinging a fifty-pound stone ball five hundred feet. Alexander's father Philip had been the first to use them in eastern Greece and while the torsion pressure of the machines was no greater than a woman's twisted braid, they transformed the art of war. Not only did they allow attacks on an enemy in the winter (when city life retreated behind its protective wall) but they also

The 'Alexander Sarcophagus'. Alexander as Great King of Persia reorganised the satrapies of the Persian Empire. One of the governors he appointed was Abdalonymus, who was installed as king in Sidon in 332 and for whom this sarcophagus was built. Alexander seems to have had a close relationship with this Phoenician.

122

marked a significant advance in an age of primitive technology. Bolts and screws were unknown. There was no rope, twine, springs or adhesive materials. No lubricants. Soda and oil were used to clean cloth, but there was no soap. Pulleys and gears were little understood. Twenty-seven years after this siege of Tyre, the ultimate siege machine was invented for an attack on Rhodes. It was nine storeys high topped with a wooden platform 30 feet on a side, but it required 3,400 men to move and operate it.

Here at Tyre Alexander made his own contribution to siege warfare. He had two 150-foot towers built, which were taller than any structures yet known. On top were catapult machines and all down the sides were animal hides to deflect fire from the wooden structure. But the Tyrians set a boat filled with combustible material ablaze which was pushed towards the towers and engulfed them in flame. So Alexander had the causeway widened for more towers to be built. All of this took time, though the causeway, once it was built, became a permanent feature that still connects Tyre to the mainland. Months passed while Alexander tried some other ploys, like mounting machines on boats, against which the Tyrians successfully used incendiary missiles. The Tyrians dropped large rocks to capsize the small Macedonian fleet. When the rocks made the area around the island too shallow, Alexander tried to dislodge them. He improvised dredging equipment, but the Tyrians cut the cables of the transport ships, using their armoured ships and then, when Alexander used armoured ships too, with divers. Finally Alexander resorted to chains, which the Tyrians could not cut, and Alexander was again able to approach close to the city wall.

During the spring of 332 two significant events occurred. Darius sent Alexander a peace offer, hoping that the Macedonians' ambitions were already sated. There had been a first peace offer while the Macedonian army was on its way to Tyre, soon after the battle of Issus. The terms of that offer are unknown, but they are assumed to be similar to this second embassy at Tyre, where Darius offered Alexander one of his daughters in marriage, the territory west of the Euphrates and ten thousand talents. To the offer Alexander made the contemptuous reply that he could marry Darius' daughter without her father's permission; and the treasures and territories were already his. Still, Parmenio said that if he were Alexander he would accept the offer. Alexander replied scornfully that if he were Parmenio, so would he. This rift may have reflected the more modest ambitions that Philip and the generals of his generation, like Parmenio, might have had. It certainly indicated a breach between the older soldiers in Alexander's army and their younger colleagues, led by Alexander himself.

At about the same time as the peace offer, Alexander won the allegiance of Phoenician ships which had been an essential part of Darius' navy. Like the Tyrians themselves, the Phoenician naval leaders had assumed that Darius would come to the aid of Tyre and repulse the Macedonian attack. The navy's inactivity as it awaited Darius was increasingly embarrassing, since Darius made no move to help Tyre. So it offered itself to Alexander, thereby assuring his eventual victory at Tyre – but not yet.

He still had to find the chink in the Tyrian armour. Ramming logs were mounted on ships so the Macedonians could probe the wall around the whole periphery of the island. In some places the wall was 150 feet high, but the Macedonians did find one place where they could break down a part of it. The Tyrians mounted their resources at the spot and repulsed the attempt to use boarding bridges to enter the city. Three days later Alexander tried again at the same place. This time he had two ships with gangways filled with infantry and the shield-bearing hypaspists. This turned into the climactic battle in August 332. An extensive section of the wall was battered down. The ships moved adjacent to the place and the soldiers put the gangways on the rubble. The first wave of attackers was stopped by the city's defenders, but Alexander led the second attempt, which took the wall, and entered the city. At the same time the Phoenician fleet attacked at the harbour and pushed the Tyrians back on the defensive. And to make a triple-sided attack, a battalion of infantry entered the city over the causeway. It was a short finale to a seven-month siege. The defenders tried to barricade the streets but attackers massed in from all directions. Those in the shrine of Agenor were forced to flee, and the Macedonians lashed out in indiscriminate slaughter. Seven thousand were murdered defending their city, while Alexander had two thousand men of military age crucified, and sold the rest of the population – thirty thousand – into slavery. The butchery was as swift and brutal as the siege was long and painstaking, a contrast that has been used to excuse Alexander's excesses. But only four

The alabaster sphinx at
Memphis, the age-old
capital of Egypt where
Alexander was installed
as pharaoh.

hundred Macedonian soldiers died throughout the Tyre campaign. Finally Alexander had his prayer at the Temple of Heracles and set off towards Egypt.

The last obstacle before reaching Egypt was the city of Gaza, ruled by King Batis who would not surrender to Alexander. Two miles inland from the coast, it could not be bypassed because it blocked the road through the Sinai. Alexander mounted another siege. This one was much shorter, but it held the same fate for its inhabitants, with all men slaughtered and the rest of the population sold into slavery. In addition, the city was turned into a Macedonian fortress repopulated with neighbouring tribesmen and troops of Alexander's. It has been stated that Alexander, angered at being delayed on his way to Egypt, had Batis hitched to his chariot, while he dragged him live around the city.

Egypt provided Alexander with his opportunity to celebrate. Its defending troops had been mutilated at Issus, along with the Egyptian satraps, so there was no need for the Macedonians to fight their way into the country. Moreover, the Egyptian people saw Alexander more as a saviour than an invader. Egypt had fallen under Persian rule only twenty years before, after a sixty-year span when Greek mercenaries had helped it maintain its independence. The offences of the Persian conquerors – desecrating temples and roasting the sacred Apis calf – made Alexander a welcome deliverer. For not only did he respect other people's religious practices, but he also showed an interest in the Egyptian gods, one of whom he was to search out in the desert. At Memphis, Alexander was enthroned as pharaoh and was later to appear in hieroglyphic texts adorned with royal titles. Extensive festivals were held, with athletes and poets brought specially from Greece.

At the end of the festivities, in the beginning of 331, Alexander left the major body of his troops behind as he undertook two projects that he had been planning. Travelling down the Nile with only his closest Companions and bodyguard, he sailed north-west towards the spot that was to become the famous city of Alexandria. Whether he stopped now or later to mark out the foundation of the city is in dispute. His next stop was farther west, in the Libyan desert, and so he may well have returned this way.

That further journey was to the oasis of Siwah, the site of the oracle of Ammon. Alexander was anxious for predictions

BELOW The remains of the ancient citadel of Siwah, and the oracular shrine of Ammon-Ra, held to be the physical father of the pharaoh. Ammon-Ra's 'sons' built temples in honour of their father, and he in turn led them to military victory. Alexander went through a ceremony which gave him rebirth as son of the god and entitled him to wear the curved ram's horns of Ammon.

of successes to come, having already been so satisfied with the Delphic oracle's pronouncements. Much myth surrounds the visit, for Alexander approached the Siwah oracle alone and later wrote to his mother that he would have to tell her what was said in person, but he never had the chance. Still, writers on Alexander have found in this visit a perfect opportunity to endow Alexander with all the attributes only an oracle could know. Questions of Alexander's paternity – the possibility being that he could have had the god Ammon for a father – the future course of the expedition and the prospects for the new city were all questions that exercised the imaginations of Alexander's admirers.

RIGHT Isis with Horus on her lap. As pharaoh Alexander was the recognised representative of god on earth. He was hailed as Horus, divine son of Ra, whose worship had prevailed in Lower Egypt, and as the son of Ammon, creator of the universe, whose worship had flourished in Upper Egypt and grown to incorporate the worship of the more southerly sun-god Ra.

Conquest of Egypt

Though Alexander spent only a short time in Egypt, his acceptance was immediate and profound. He responded to this by rebuilding the temples which the Persians had destroyed.

RIGHT The Temple of Luxor, the southern part of the ruins of ancient Thebes. Built by Amenhotep III and dedicated partly to Mut, wife of Ammon, the sanctuary was restored by Alexander.

OPPOSITE ABOVE The hypostyle in the Great Temple of Ammon-Ra at Karnak. Completed and decorated by Rameses II, it was the largest columned hall ever constructed. OPPOSITE BELOW Part of the avenue of ram-headed sphinxes leading to the Great Temple of Ammon-Ra at Karnak, near Thebes. The spirit of Ammon-Ra dwelt in the ram-headed sphinx which combined the solar sphinx with the ram symbol of fertility sacred to Ammon.

He might have felt that the founding of this new city required a respectful visit to the oracle of Ammon, which would have been reason enough for the trek in the desert. He was leaving nothing amiss in the enterprise. Unlike most of Alexander's foundations, of which there may have been as many as seventy – though most of them soon disappeared – this one was to be a commercial centre rather than a garrison town. A military depot would have been more appropriate farther east and inland, while this location had the makings of an ideal port and link between Greece and the East. Plutarch reports that another site had already been chosen when Alexander had a dream in which he remembered the lines of Homer in the *Odyssey*:

Out of the tossing sea where it breaks on the beaches of Egypt
Rises an isle from the waters: the name that men give it is Pharos.

After inspecting the site, Alexander was said to have remarked that Homer, besides his known qualities, had the instincts of an architect.

Alexander had the city laid out in a radial manner, similar to what was considered a modern design when Washington D.C. was designed some two thousand years later. Another story from Plutarch relates that Alexander marked out the boundaries of the city with bags of barley grain, for lack of anything better. When birds came and ate all the grain, Alexander was alarmed, but he was reassured by the seers' interpretation that the new city would have ample resources of its own and supply the needs of many peoples besides. It did more than fulfil its function to supplant Tyre, for it became the central trading port of the world in the years after Alexander's death. The East-West cross-fertilisation in which Alexander showed so much interest was well served by the city he founded. Later to become the capital of the Ptolemaic Empire and the place where Alexander himself was buried it was one of the most enduring tributes to the king and his expedition. In the harbour was the island Pharos which he had connected to the shore by a causeway and given a 150-foot-high lighthouse. In some languages the word for lighthouse or lantern is a variation on 'pharos', a continuing reminder of Alexander's contribution.

To make Egypt easily manageable, Alexander had it sub-divided into numerous units. Under the Persians, there were already Upper and Lower satrapies, one of these being the domain of the kingmaker eunuch, Bagoas. Alexander made further divisions: between civil and military authority, east and west frontier commands, and even within the army, mercenary and garrison commands. The leaders of each of these units could keep watch over the others to prevent concerted revolt from this, the largest of Alexander's conquests. For convenience, Cleomenes, the commander of the eastern military district, was authorised to collect the tribute from the Upper and Lower satraps, but in time this small advantage gave Cleomenes the necessary foothold to gain control over all of Egypt. The system worked sufficiently well at the beginning to suit Alexander's needs.

From Egypt, Alexander returned to Tyre, where he spent the summer of 331 before continuing farther east. Here too he established a rudimentary government, whose main purpose was the collection of tribute and the maintenance of peace. One of its accomplishments was to issue a standardised currency which Alexander was anxious to have. While in Tyre he received an embassy from Athens requesting the release of the mercenaries condemned to forced labour in Macedonia after their defeat two years earlier at Granicus. This time he granted their release, possibly in reaction to the news, which came at about this time, that Agis of Sparta was leading a revolt in Greece. Supported by the Thracian king, Agis was hoping for support from Athens, but the city was willing to put its trust in Alexander's leniency. In withholding its navy's four hundred ships from the rebels, Athens was indeed entitled to the release of the mercenaries. Though the rebel force totalled some thirty thousand men, Alexander confidently assumed that Antipater would be able to handle them. Yet the situation was not to be resolved for some months, during which Alexander was preoccupied with another matter: the second confrontation with Darius.

6 The Roa

Persepolis

HAVING SETTLED THE AFFAIRS of his conquered territories, Alexander set out from Tyre in the late spring
of 331. The next time he was this far west would be as a
corpse being taken to Egypt, but for the moment Alexander
had no thought of death for his expedition had all the
auguries of success.

Plutarch tells that on the initial stages of the march the
army's camp followers became increasingly involved in a
mock battle taking the sides of Alexander's army and Darius'.
The amusement got to the stage of stone-throwing and club-
bing, when Alexander took an interest in it and gave weapons
and armour to his namesake in the fray. Philotas outfitted the
so-called Darius who fought 'Alexander' in single combat
which 'the whole army watched and saw in it something of an
omen for their own campaign', Plutarch relates. 'After a
strenuous fight "Alexander" finally prevailed and got as a
reward twelve villages and the right to wear the Persian dress.'
Then there was an eclipse of the moon, which was also taken
as a sign of impending success.

Alexander was transporting a larger force than the one
which had fought at the initial battle at Granicus. Now some
forty thousand strong in infantry and seven thousand in
cavalry, the army was to travel more than three thousand miles
in eighteen months. Averaging ten miles a day, as opposed to
the Persian army's maximum of seven miles, Alexander was
fast approaching his climactic battle with the Great King of
Persia.

What Darius lacked in mobility he made up for in size. In
the two years since Issus, he had managed to amass at Babylon
another army, this one centred on a cavalry of thirty-five
thousand – five times larger than Alexander's. With this new
force and a patient strategy of drawing Alexander into battle,
he gave every indication of having learned from his previous
humiliation.

A small Persian force of three thousand was sent out to
follow Alexander's progress towards Babylon. The most
direct route, which follows the Euphrates River south-east for
450 miles, had the added advantage of supporting a narrow
band of vegetation in the river valley. But Persia's scouting
party was capable of laying waste the area ahead of
Alexander's march. Besides, there was the considerable element of surprise in taking an unexpected route. So, instead of
marching downstream as predicted, the Macedonians headed

PREVIOUS PAGES Soldiers
marching in formation,
a detail from the Nereid
Monument of Xanthus in
Lycia, fourth century BC.

136

Greeks fighting Amazons
from the Mausoleum at
Halicarnassus.

across the Mesopotamian plain. They crossed the Euphrates
in late July or early August, using two bridges built by
Hephaestion, and marched north-east.

They marched unopposed through Mesopotamia. The
route, which in fact moved away from Babylon, was one
indication of Alexander's attempt to draw Darius away from
his stronghold. Another was the slow progress of the Macedonian circling motion. Lacking precise information on the
dating of the journey and the place the army crossed the
Tigris, it is impossible to know the exact length of the march,
but for an army capable of doing ten miles a day, it certainly
went no faster than eight and a half, and possibly only five and
and a half miles a day. The strategy worked. Not only was the
Persian army drawn out, but Darius then proceeded at a considerably greater speed than Alexander, hoping that the scouts
would engage the Macedonian army at the Tigris, with the
full body of Darius' attack weighing in to prevent the invaders

137

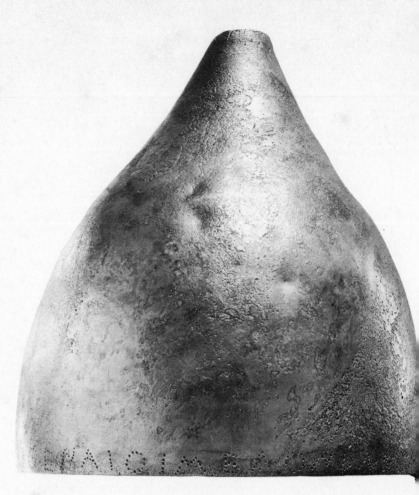

A Persian helmet
found at Olympia.

from crossing the river. But the farther north Alexander
crossed the Tigris, the farther Darius had to march to meet
him. The most likely crossings – both of them north of the
ultimate battle site at Gaugamela – were farther from Babylon
than Alexander had come from the Euphrates.

Darius missed catching Alexander's army crossing the
river, and so he stopped at a site eighty miles south of there.
After being hemmed in at Issus, he stayed on a wide plain,
which could accommodate his cavalry and chariots – and one
that was coincidentally near Nineveh where three hundred
years earlier the Assyrians had lost the same Persian Empire
to Darius' antecedents. Alexander knew from captives
that Darius' army was camped at the plain and decided to
rest his own troops seven miles away. A hill between the
armies prevented their seeing each other, but after four days'
rest, Alexander marched his army to the top of the hill,

where Darius' overwhelming force could be seen three miles in the distance.

Darius had made prodigious preparations for this battle. His cavalry were given better arms, more in line with Macedonian weapons: their javelins were replaced with large swords and short thrusting spears, as well as link armour. The chosen plain at Gaugamela was flattened out even more by his own troops, making a surface seven miles wide. The total number of his troops is unknown. Ancient sources put it in grossly exaggerated figures at about a million. The fact was that he had thirty-five thousand in the cavalry. His infantry had been wiped out at Issus. It would have been extremely difficult to recruit a new infantry to the standard of Alexander's, but he also must have felt there was no need for one. He also outfitted two hundred four-horse chariots equipped with long spears in front and cutting scythes behind (a machine that had proved itself to be of little use in the past).

More important, he had adapted his strategy to meet Alexander's order of battle at Granicus and Issus. Opposite the Macedonian right wing (the offensive side led by Alexander himself) were a hundred of the chariots and a group of crack infantry to absorb Alexander's attack. On the other Persian wing was Mazaeus, the Babylonian satrap and leader of their scouting party. He had previously fought in the same formation against the Thessalians, who were not likely to forget his formidable opposition. The Persian line was so long that Alexander had to adapt the second line of his phalanx to be able to turn around in case of being outflanked, making a square formation to confront the surrounding Persians.

Darius' confinement to the plain gave Alexander complete discretion on when to attack. He rejected the advice of the majority of officers to make an immediate attack at night. Instead, he followed Parmenio's counsel to wait until he had undertaken careful reconnaissance. Alexander himself took his light cavalry on an extended mission, which the Persians left unmolested. In this situation the advantage of surprise in an immediate attack was far outweighed by the disadvantage of fighting at night; the brute strength of Darius' forces had to be countered with a carefully controlled battle order, which Alexander had to be able to oversee throughout the battle. 'I will not steal my victory like a thief in the night' is Plutarch's memorable version of Alexander's reasoning, but it hardly accords with the careful preparations that were required against this imposing enemy.

Darius had absorbed the strategic lessons of his previous defeats, but he was still intent on relying on overwhelming strength of numbers to blanket any move of Alexander's. The actual vulnerability of this posture was apparent even before the fighting began. Darius' men had to stand at the ready the whole night while Alexander's troops slept. Alexander is said to have slept particularly well himself. When finally awakened after all his men had breakfasted, he commented, 'Why not sleep well? Do you not see that we have already won the battle, now that we are delivered from roving around these endless devastated plains, and chasing this Darius, who will never stand and fight?'

Nevertheless, for all those loftily confident words, he is sure to have spent a great deal of time going over plans and contingency measures. The size of his Companions compared to the Persian cavalry was an obvious cause for concern, since he was particularly sensitive to strengths and weaknesses in numbers. Though he must have toyed with the idea of switching his offensive unit from the right flank to the left, his final deployment looked conventional – though it held a surprise for Darius.

The set speeches provided by Alexander's biographers tend to be their own imaginations at work, but Arrian's report of Alexander's last exhortation to his officers mentions an uncommon item. Alexander emphasises the need 'to preserve discipline in the hour of danger, to advance – when told to do so – in utter silence. . . . All must obey orders promptly and pass them on without hesitation to the men.' Alexander was soon to demonstrate the reason for requiring strict discipline and emphasising this seemingly elementary point.

Each side wanted the other to be drawn into battle, but the war of nerves broke with Darius making the first contact. Three thousand Persian forces were ordered to stop the lateral movement of Alexander's men trying to outflank Darius' enormous line. Alexander answered with only six hundred men. Then another eight thousand Persian soldiers attacked and for a time were held by the far inferior force of one thousand one hundred and ten Macedonian light cavalry and six thousand seven hundred infantry. This force that was supposed to absorb Alexander's attack was in fact itself being heavily engaged attacking a small element of the Macedonian offensive side.

At this point, Darius let go with the chariots. Alexander had taken the precaution of arranging for the lines to break for the chariots to go through, a highly unorthodox move. Darius then began his major charge. Thinking that the major Macedonian force had already been engaged, he was not concerned about the decreasing depth of his formation, which had been caused by Alexander's shifting. There was in fact a dangerous breach between the wing encircling Alexander's right-hand side and the centre of the Persian forces. Darius' charge was met with the front line of Alexander's javelins. When the dust had cleared, the breach in the Persian line was obvious.

As the Persians charged and revealed the gap in their line, Alexander charged with his right wing. Alexander's attacking force comprised eight squadrons of Companions organised in a wedge. In one long sentence, Arrian – our one source on this – makes short shrift of the conclusive phase of the battle:

A close struggle ensued, but it was soon over; for when the Macedonian horses, with Alexander himself at the head of them, vigorously pressed the assault, fighting hand to hand and thrusting at the Persians' faces with their spears, and the infantry phalanx in close order and bristling with pikes added its irresistible weight, Darius, who had been on edge since the battle began and now saw nothing but terror all around him, was the first to turn tail and ride for safety.

The battle, however, was not over. As before, Alexander felt it wiser to conclude the fighting before chasing Darius, since the throne of Persia was now his anyway. An urgent message from Parmenio on the other flank brought Alexander's forces to bolster that side against the formidable opposition of Mazaeus. At the time of the Persian central attack, Darius sent a group of about five hundred special forces to recapture the Persian royal family behind the Macedonian line. The forces got through and caused some consternation among Alexander's troops, but they were soon overpowered.

Intense fighting was still maintained by the Persian forces

anxious to avoid being encircled by the victorious Macedonians. Sixty of the Companions including Hephaestion were injured, but the vanquished were eventually allowed to flee. Alexander's troops then followed in hot pursuit, unwilling to waste any advantage of the decisive victory. Parmenio and his men stayed behind with the Persian booty.

Alexander's pursuit of Darius lasted only the seventy-five miles from the battlefield to Arbela. At that juncture, Darius fled eastward over the Kurdish mountains to Media. Alexander then returned to distribute Darius' war chest among his troops, who got from two to ten months' extra pay. As Darius expected, the Macedonian army proceeded leisurely and regally down to Babylon instead of chasing him. There Alexander anticipated resistance from Mazaeus, who had retreated from his protracted battle with the Thessalian wing of Alexander's army back to his satrapy of Babylon. While the Macedonian troops approached the city in battle dress, Mazaeus emerged from it garbed as a suppliant. According to Aristotle, Babylon was so big that news of the surrender took two days to circulate among its inhabitants. Alexander was ceremoniously received in the city where he treated his soldiers to the lavish fruits of their victory. For a month the Macedonian troops were fêted with recreational sports, contests and orgiastic entertainment.

Alexander was welcomed by the natives. He restored the temple of their god Marduk (their name for Heracles), which Xerxes had destroyed when he took the city for the Persians. Alexander knew the resentment such destruction causes, since it was this Xerxes his father Philip had sworn to avenge in planning his campaign to Asia Minor.

The year before, the siege of Tyre was occasioned by the refusal to let Alexander offer sacrifices to the same god Marduk-Heracles; in making the sacrifices here, he was conferred with sovereignty over 'the four quarters of the globe'. Over the next few years he was gradually to adopt the trappings of the Great King, with a full-complement of concubines, eunuchs and other attendants. The fusion of his court was to cause concern and eventually revolt among some Macedonians who had been with him from the beginning. But at Babylon only the rudiments of this development were formulated and instituted.

142

Though no doubt a shock to his warriors who had just finished a fierce battle with him, Mazaeus was reappointed satrap by Alexander. It was a choice prompted by Mazaeus' cooperation in surrendering the city, but Alexander was not so much rewarding bravery or compliance as establishing a practical policy that he was to carry on elsewhere. Alexander made the bold move of dividing authority between the existing satrap and Greek or Macedonian administrators. It offered the olive branch to the native aristocracy without surrendering all authority to them. Mazaeus was granted the unique right to coin silver, a privilege he had already held as satrap but one that Alexander was to revoke from other satraps in the future. The division of power, though, was here shared between the native satrap, a Greek commander-in-chief and a Macedonian financial officer. This eventually became standard practice but it was particularly appropriate to start with Mazaeus because, though he himself was Persian, he had a Babylonian wife. Thus he had pursued his own policy of integrating cultures even before Alexander's arrival.

After a month in Babylon, it was almost winter 331 when Alexander undertook the twenty-day journey to Susa, the opulent capital of the Persian kings. The city with its fabulous palace and treasure had already been surrendered to the troops that Alexander had taken the precaution of sending direct from Gaugamela. On the way to Susa, Alexander was informed of Antipater's difficulties in Greece, caused by the revolt of Sparta. King Agis of Sparta had not supported the rest of the Greeks against Philip at the climactic battle of Chaeronea, out of which the League of Corinth was formed. Now Antipater was able to use the troops of the League against Agis, who was killed in a closely fought battle that the Spartans lost. Alexander did not hear of the successful conclusion before he reached Susa; so he sent some three thousand talents for Antipater to defend himself.

Along the route to Susa, Alexander also reorganised his army. New commands were appointed in the cavalry and light infantry as a result of the showing at Gaugamela, but also in anticipation of the rough terrain ahead, where these divisions would be put to a severe test. The Companions, in being divided into squadrons, became more flexible. Fifteen thousand reinforcements from Macedonia had just

ABOVE AND BELOW Mythical animals
moulded on to the brick walls of Babylon.
The technique employed was curious; the
whole figure was modelled in the wet
material, cut into bricks while still soft
and then glazed. Finally, the bricks were
pieced together again jig-saw fashion and
applied to the wall.
RIGHT A Persian bodyguard, in glazed
brick, from the palace at Susa.

arrived, and they were incorporated into the new formations.

As the main capital of the Persian kings, Susa held a prodigious treasure. There was supposedly five thousand talents' worth of purple cloth alone. Since the Persian kings tended to hoard their gold and let barter suffice for trade, Alexander found a mountain of ingots. Along with the solemn ceremonies and reappointment of the satrap, Alexander also installed the captured Persian royal family in Susa. Darius' wife had died earlier, but the king's mother and children were left there with instructions to be taught Greek. Now that he was King of Asia, Alexander was deliberately embarking on a course of assimilation, which on his return seven years later would result in a huge ceremony of mixed marriages – including his own.

While Darius continued eastward across northern Asia, Alexander continued to ignore him and move farther south from Susa to Persepolis. The ceremonial centre of the Persian Empire, Persepolis boasted a Great Temple, on which were written in cuneiform the proud words: 'Thus saith King Darius: this land of Persia, which Ahuramazda has granted me, which is fair, rich in men and rich in horses, according to the will of Ahuramazda and of me King Darius, trembles before no enemy.'

The road to this prize presented two last obstacles, the first of which was minor enough to show the sheer obstinacy and thoroughness of Alexander's adventurous conquests. Though the Persian kings had been willing to pay a tribute to the mountaineer guardians of a high pass between Susa and Persepolis, Alexander was not. With the quick cavalry which he had detailed to go with him, he reached the pass and told the native Uxians that he would pay the customary tribute. Then with the native guides Alexander always used in unfamiliar terrain, he circled round the back of the pass and scared the frightened guardians into the hands of the squadrons waiting on the other side. Having killed off a number of villagers on his way and slaughtered the guardians of the pass, Alexander was at least persuaded by the Persian queen mother not to take their territory away from them. Instead, they had to pay a heavy tribute consisting of a hundred horses a year, five hundred mules and thirty thousand sheep because they had no currency.

An aerial view of ancient Susa: to the left, the Kerkha River,
in antiquity the Choaspes. The mound was occupied from
prehistoric times. Darius took up residence here in 521 BC and
carried out extensive building projects, later destroyed by Xerxes
Alexander entered Susa, unopposed, and spared the city.

The other obstacle on the way to Persepolis was created by a Persian satrap who occupied the narrow Persian Gates with a force of more than twenty-five thousand. For this formidable opposition, Alexander used basically the same technique, having learned the way around from captured prisoners. Strategically it was the only possible action but with typical thoroughness Alexander had also arranged precise timing for a concerted attack and for troops to surround the enemy and prevent escape. It was also no mean feat negotiating around the enemy without being detected. The resulting carnage was only a brief but dramatic diversion on the way to Persepolis.

Still, Alexander felt compelled to reach the city and its treasure in the greatest haste for fear of their being destroyed before his arrival. He was accepted into the city without opposition and, as before, he reappointed the Persian satrap. The hoards of wealth found there were equal to his expectations and were on the same scale as the amounts accumulated in the other places where the Persian kings spent any time.

Alexander's own booty was said to require two thousand pairs of mules and five hundred camels to carry it away. Though he had not yet killed or captured Darius, there was no doubt at this point – halfway in time and distance towards his final destination in the Punjab – that he had assumed the place of the Great King of Persia. It is therefore a continuing mystery to historians and biographers why Alexander allowed his troops to plunder Persepolis and why he himself had the Great Palace of Xerxes burned to the ground. The plundering at least rewarded an army that had been driven hard and was expecting a handsome reward. The previous restraint was less characteristic of victorious invaders than the present indulgence.

When soldiers forced their way into the Great Palace they toppled a gigantic statue of Xerxes, which Alexander later came upon. He was said to have looked down on the head and spoken to it as if it were alive: 'Shall I pass by and leave you lying there because of the expedition you led against Greece, or shall I set you up again because of your magnanimity and your virtues in other respects?' He left the pieces on the ground – and was to show even greater disrespect for this ruler and the notion of kingly virtue.

According to Arrian, 'Parmenio urged Alexander to

149

LEFT An immense double-headed capital, now fallen to the ground.
BELOW LEFT Relief from Persepolis of an Armenian envoy bringing tribute to the Great King at the time of the New Year Festival.

TOP RIGHT Capital of a lion's head.
BELOW One of the gates of the Chamber of One Hundred Columns. Darius is portrayed at the top, enthroned in regal splendour.

spare the Great Palace for several reasons, chiefly because it was hardly wise to destroy what was now his own property, and because the Asians would, in his opinion, be less willing to support him if he seemed bent merely on passing through their country as a conqueror rather than ruling it as a king.' Arrian says that Alexander replied that he wanted to avenge the Persian invasion of Greece, but Arrian himself considered that a bad policy as 'it could hardly be considered as punishment for Persians long dead and gone'. There are scholars who agree that Alexander was preoccupied with showing the Greeks that, in burning the palace, he was still their leader and avenger.

The final possible answer, believed by Plutarch among others, seems the most plausible because it has the least reason behind it. At a drunken revelry, perhaps as part

Aerial view of the Caspian
Gates.

of a *komos* – a dance in honour of Dionysus – a celebrated
Athenian courtesan named Thais raised a toast in which
she said, 'It would be an even sweeter pleasure to end the
party by going out and setting fire to the palace of Xerxes,
who had laid Athens in ashes.' On impulse Alexander agreed
and, according to this version, encouraged later rationalisa-
tions to cover his regret at what he had thoughtlessly
allowed.

After four months in Persepolis, Alexander headed north
towards Ecbatana, the old capital of Media. This was the
central communications centre of the Persian Empire as
well as Darius' refuge. In the six months since Gaugamela,
Darius had managed to accumulate only six thousand
infantry and three thousand cavalry. Hoping that Darius
would stay there to fight, and laden with the vast entourage
that his successes had attracted, Alexander slowly made for
the Great King's retreat.

When Alexander got near Ecbatana (present-day Hamadan),
he heard that Darius had fled north-eastward towards the
Caspian Gates. With the troops he had recruited, Darius was
intending to defend the gates. So Alexander rushed with his
troops, leaving the entourage to trail behind. Reaching
Ecbatana in mid-June, he delayed long enough to make
certain arrangements before chasing the Persian king.
Among the arrangements was the declaration that the
original Pan-Hellenic crusade against the Persian Empire was
now finished. Henceforth Alexander would be acting as
king of Macedonia and Persia and no longer as head of the
League of Corinth – not that it was a difference of substance.
The allied Greek troops were dismissed with handsome
remuneration, but they were invited to reenlist with the
inducement of a large payment for those who remained.
Many did and the rest were to be escorted back to Greece.
Harpalus, a lifelong friend and Companion of Alexander's,
was appointed royal treasurer, entrusted with the huge sum
of 180,000 talents. Parmenio was sent off with a contingent
to subdue the Cadusians, who had been allies of Darius and
were expected to contribute troops against Alexander. The
old general had served Alexander well, but the king was no
doubt relieved to establish his authority without the
continued presence of the most powerful of the older
generation of Macedonian nobility.

153

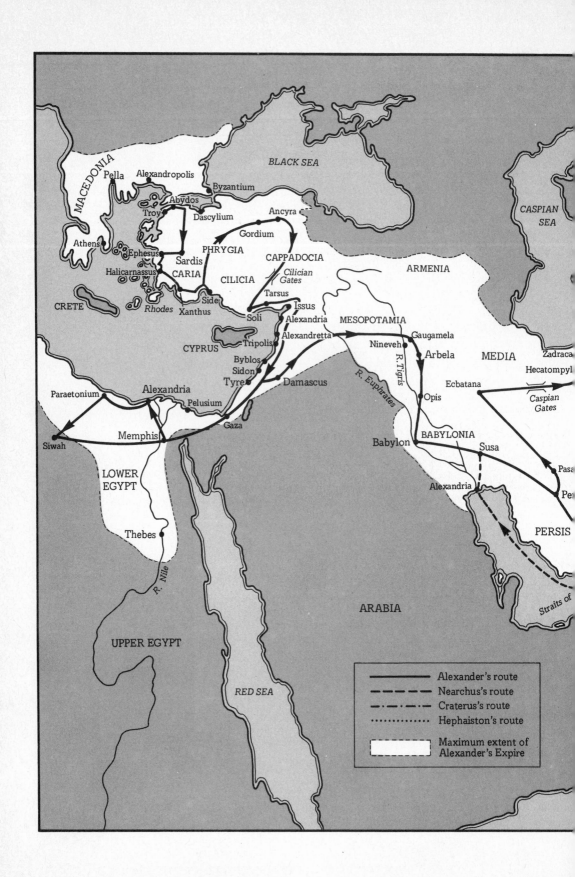

BLACK SEA

MACEDONIA

Pella
Alexandropolis
Byzantium
Abydos
Troy
Dascylium
Ancyra
Gordium
Athens
PHRYGIA
CAPPADOCIA
Ephesus
Sardis
CARIA
Halicarnassus
CILICIA
Cilician
Gates
CRETE
Side
Tarsus
Rhodes
Xanthus
Soli
Issus
Alexandria
MESOPOTAMIA
CYPRUS
Tripolis
Alexandretta
Nineveh
Byblos
Sidon
Tyre
Damascus
Gaugamela
Arbela
MEDIA
Zadraca
Hecatompyl
R. Euphrates
R. Tigris
Ecbatana
Paraetonium
Alexandria
Opis
Caspian
Gates
Pelusium
Gaza
Memphis
Babylon
BABYLONIA
Susa
Siwah
Pasa
LOWER
EGYPT
Alexandria
Pe
Thebes
PERSIS

ARMENIA

CASPIAN
SEA

R. Nile

ARABIA

Straits of

UPPER EGYPT

RED SEA

——————— Alexander's route
– – – – – Nearchus's route
–·–·–·– Craterus's route
·········· Hephaiston's route
Maximum extent of
Alexander's Expire

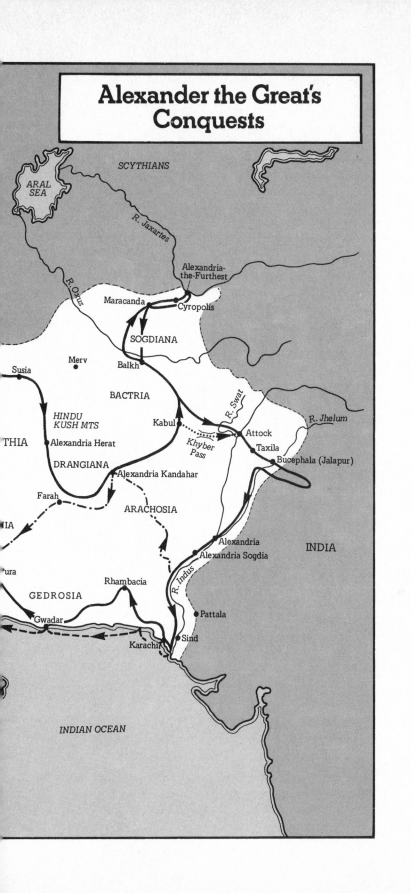

Alexander the Great's Conquests

SCYTHIANS

ARAL SEA

R. Jaxartes

R. Oxus

Alexandria-the-Furthest

Maracanda

Cyropolis

SOGDIANA

Merv

Balkh

Susia

BACTRIA

R. Swat

HINDU KUSH MTS

Kabul

R. Jhelum

THIA

Alexandria Herat

Attock

Khyber Pass

Taxila

DRANGIANA

Bucephala (Jalapur)

Alexandria Kandahar

Farah

ARACHOSIA

IA

Alexandria

INDIA

Alexandria Sogdia

ura

R. Indus

Rhambacia

GEDROSIA

Gwadar

Pattala

Karachi

Sind

INDIAN OCEAN

Darius had a five-day head start on Alexander. The hand-picked troops with Alexander made a furious eleven-day race towards Rhagae (near present-day Teheran) where they rested for five days. Many of the troops were too exhausted or slow to carry on. Alexander learned from deserters that the Persian king had been arrested by his followers. Alexander lost no time pursuing them, making a two-day journey in which his men rested only in the midday heat. They came upon Darius' last known camp and found Darius' old interpreter who told the story of the king's stumbling fortunes. Open revolt had broken out in the Persian camp, with two satraps, Bessus and Nabarzanes, intent on taking over from the weak and ineffectual king. They managed to imprison Darius when his loyal Persian troops saw the futility of their resistance against Alexander. As the Persian army moved eastward, Darius was held in a wagon, with Alexander fearful that he might abdicate in favour of Bessus in order to save his own life.

It was clear there was no time to lose. Overnight, Alexander led a group of sixty light cavalry through forty miles of deserted sand flats. At dawn they spotted the caravan of carts in the distance. The pursuit ended in frustration, for Darius was not found among the group. Then one of Alexander's officers, searching for water, found an abandoned wagon, its team unhitched. Inside was Darius, bound in gold chains – dead. His killers had escaped on horseback and Alexander remained to wrap the king in his own cloak. Alexander took the mantle of rightful succession by condemning the murderers to death and having Darius' body shipped back to Persepolis for a royal funeral and interment in the dynastic crypt.

Darius' brother was given the honour, unique for an oriental, of being appointed one of Alexander's Companions, and the royal entourage took on more trappings of the new empire, including Persian dress and ceremony. Though Alexander still had to fight his way, area by area, through the East, he had now fulfilled his (and his father's) original ambition. But ambition now took on a greater scope, which became more obsessive as it became ever more successful.

7 Only a God

IN 330 ALEXANDER, now aged twenty-six, had conquered more territory than any European in history. His exploits on three continents had already earned his place in history as well as legend, but there was no reason to assume that his ambition had been sated. Of course it hadn't been, and Alexander continued farther east as though Darius' death were just one more obstacle surmounted.

The nature of the expedition, however, was gradually and perceptibly changing. In Ecbatana, Alexander had already abandoned the pretence of pursuing Pan-Greek interests as hegemon of the League of Corinth. At the time of Darius' death, when the Macedonian army was just below the Caspian Sea in the middle of Asia, it became apparent that Alexander had no intention of going back to Europe at all. Not only did he continue his adoption of royal Persian customs, but he was also incorporating Persian soldiers into his army.

The proliferating Asian Alexandrias, now being established in earnest because of the need for garrisons and communications centres, were being settled with mixtures of Greek and native peoples. Recruitment had been going on in Greece and Macedonia for the specific purpose of manning the new cities and there is every reason to attribute to Alexander the intention of creating a multiracial social order – created by and loyal to him. We are inclined to rate Alexander as an open-minded humanitarian for such an undertaking, especially in an age of such unabashed prejudice as that expressed by Aristotle. But whatever the humanitarian grounds for Alexander's actions, he also had the distinct and cogent strategy of ending his own dependence on Greek, Macedonian or Persian societies by creating his own. As Plutarch put it, 'He believed that his authority would be more securely established if the two traditions could be blended and assimilated.'

The danger of any dependence, especially on his Macedonian nobles, was also becoming evident as Alexander moved farther into Asia. The last threat to Alexander's life had been at the time of his illness before the battle at Issus, when he let his doctor read the warning against an elixir that Alexander was nonetheless drinking at that very moment. This confidence in his colleagues, supposedly a sign of the secure king rather than the fearful tyrant, was never misplaced, and no threat to the king's life had been

PREVIOUS PAGES
Alexander appears
wearing the attributes
of several deities. The
elephant scalp belongs
to Dionysus, the mythical
conqueror of India; below
the edge of the scalp is seen
the tip of the ram's horn
of Zeus Ammon.

LEFT Alexander has remained
an inspiration to artists
throughout the centuries.
His magnificence is shown
here in an Indian miniature
depicting Alexander
and Roxane.

reported since that episode in 333. But from 330, there was a succession of difficulties with the Macedonians and Greeks of the original entourage.

A major source of the problem was Alexander's growing suspicions and automatic defensiveness. When he reacted with impetuous draconian measures to the report of new conspiracies against his life, he no doubt put his nobles on guard and heightened the tensions that must now have been growing at court. It was soon after Darius' death, as the Macedonian troops were passing through Parthia, that Alexander first adopted Asian dress. Though Plutarch takes pains to emphasise the limited extent of this innovation (not wearing the tiara with its conical cloth wound like a turban, nor the baggy trousers or sleeved vest), it was no doubt a shock to the Macedonian troops. In fact, Alexander held two separate courts, with the trappings of Persian royalty evident only to Asians. For a long time only the closest of his Macedonian friends could see the King of Asia in his new role, but by this very honour he was distinguishing his nearer friends from the body of soldiers and even leaders of the Macedonians. The rise of Hephaestion's influence has been marked from this time, when no longer would the military commanders be the men closest to the king. Plutarch relates the ill will that existed between Hephaestion and Craterus, who became the second in command when Parmenio was left at Ecbatana. In one argument the two came to blows, which Alexander himself had to break up, swearing that he loved both men more than any other human beings. At the same time he told them he would kill them both – or at least the one who started it – were they to fight again. Henceforth the two men desisted from their quarrelling, but they continued to represent the divisions that were threatening the court. Not that Alexander was ever ashamed of the divisions he was causing, for 'he often said that Hephaestion was a friend of Alexander's while Craterus was a friend of the king', as Plutarch relates.

These civil problems only enhanced Alexander's unforeseen military obstacles. He was entering vast plains ringed with deserts and mountains. The weather was like nothing he or his men had ever seen, with snow so deep in winter that the army was lucky to find shelter in huts that were completely submerged in the snow. Moreover, the natives put up tenacious and resourceful resistance. Alexander had not properly gauged their fighting abilities and knowledgable advantage in the rugged terrain.

He was deceived in part by the ease with which he conquered Darius' entourage after the king himself was dead. They had fled to Tapuria, a land on the southern coast of the Caspian Sea. When Alexander chased them there, they put up no resistance and he showed leniency towards them. Even Nabarzanes, one of Darius' murderers, was pardoned, an act that contradicted the previous determination to avenge Darius' death. His leniency may have been due to the satraps' gift to Alexander of a eunuch (allowing one of the few speculations that can be made about Alexander's sexual practices). The king, however, was still just following the precedent of leaving compliant satraps with their previous authority.

Subduing the Mardians, a strong warrior tribe west of Tapuria, proved more difficult. The archers who lived in this mountainous area had played an important part in Darius' army and were renowned for their courage. Since Alexander had already bypassed them in going to Tapuria, they were caught by surprise when he did attack. Those who fled to the hills did not expect Alexander to follow in pursuit, but, when he did, they surrendered unconditionally. Alexander put the territory under the control of one of the satraps he had found in Tapuria, thus ending the proud independence of the Mardians.

The mercenaries Alexander found at Tapuria were not treated tolerantly either. Choosing once more to act as hegemon of the League of Corinth, he excused only those mercenaries who had joined Darius' army before the forma- tion of the League. The others had to do the remainder of their service with Alexander. Envoys from Sparta and Athens were also found among the captured at Tapuria and were put under arrest.

Alexander's troubles began not in Tapuria, but with the escape of Bessus, another of Darius' killers. He claimed the Persian throne for himself, changing his name to Artaxerxes as he headed east. Had Darius been captured alive, he could have ordained Alexander as his successor and pre- vented any rivalry. As it was, Bessus inspired an uprising which gathered strength even after he himself was captured.

163

A satrap receiving the surrender of a city, a detail from the Xanthus Nereid monument in Lycia.

It was no surprise that Bessus led a revolt, since he was being hunted as a killer of Darius. But his supporters, who included satraps Alexander had shown favour to, ostensibly had no reason to rebel. The waves of resistance, which lasted three years and disastrously postponed Alexander's march into India, show the signs of incipient nationalism. A common race and their adherence to the Zoroastrian religion gave grounds for common action. Resentment against Alexander, which inspired their resistance despite his leniency, may have arisen over the burning of Persepolis. Just such a possibility had already been mooted by Parmenio at the time of the burning. Though Alexander had hoped to redress the regrettable burning, in both seeking to capture Darius alive and showing clemency towards the satraps, the people were not appeased.

In fact, Alexander never fully realised the degree of

resistance he would meet. Satibarzanes was left with his satrapy in Aria. Alexander's occupying troops consisted of only forty mounted javelin men whose function was to prevent looting and harassment from the army passing through. But Satibarzanes had no intention of complying with Alexander's rule. For his part, Alexander had just heard that Bessus was wearing the royal tiara upright, as only the Great King could do. More significantly, he was recruiting in Bactria, farther to the east. So Alexander was anxious to be able to trust Satibarzanes and leave Aria as quickly as possible.

It was not long after he left, as he was on the way to Bactria, that a messenger intercepted Alexander to tell him that Satibarzanes had killed the forty javelin men and had himself fled to join Bessus. This new force was gathering at the Arian capital of Artacoana, where Bessus was coming

with his recruited Scythians and Bactrians. Alexander left the major part of his forces with Craterus and took only the Companions and two battalions of infantry on a forced march that covered the seventy-five miles to Artacoana in only two days.

Satibarzanes was unprepared for Alexander's sudden appearance and fled to Bactria, but without his troops, who tried to escape Alexander as best they could. Alexander stayed in Aria a month. 'All who had had any hand in the revolt or had left their villages at the time of its occurrence were rapidly hunted down and rounded up in various places,' according to Arrian. Despite this, Alexander retained confidence in his own policies and appointed Arsaces, another Persian, as satrap. Instead of continuing east on the trail of Bessus and Satibarzanes, Alexander took his army south to Drangiana, just to assure peace behind him as he prepared to advance. This was the territory of Barsaentes, another of Darius' murderers, who knew his life would not be safe were he captured. He fled eastward; a tribe of Indians arrested him and sent him back to Alexander to be executed.

In Phrasia, a city in southern Drangiana, one of the most controversial and significant events of Alexander's life took place: the elimination of the two most powerful people in the Macedonian army. One, Parmenio, the former second in command, was in Ecbatana but still a man of great importance. The most senior and influential Macedonian noble, he was the leader of the old guard of soldiers who had served under Philip. The other was his son, Philotas, commander of the Companions and lifelong friend of Alexander. However, Philotas was known to object to Alexander's recent assimilation of Persian customs. Moreover, he and his father knew that they had the support of the rest of the Macedonian nobility and army should a confrontation arise with Alexander over the future of the campaign and the prerogatives of the king. The circumstances surrounding their deaths are clear in outline, but differ in detail depending on the historian's determination to defend Alexander. But his defenders have had to go to great lengths to exonerate him completely.

Because of the despotic turn in the Macedonian court, the elimination of Parmenio and Philotas would surely have been enticing and manageable to Alexander. Nicanor, Philotas' brother, had just died in Aria. While attending to

ABOVE Gold plate for the sheath of a Scythian sword: decoration in relief shows a contest between Greeks and barbarians (probably Persians).
LEFT Piece of a gold burial breastplate from Scythia, showing fighting beasts.

167

his funeral Philotas fell several days behind the rest of Alexander's army. If Alexander hatched a plot to frame Philotas in some way, this was the perfect time to do it.

Indeed eight days after Philotas was reunited with the army, he was accused of plotting to kill Alexander. His involvement was tenuous, for his crime was that of not passing on information that *others* were plotting against the king. Among these 'others' were an obscure Macedonian named Dimnus, his lover who betrayed him named Nicomachus, and Nicomachus' brother who had supposedly told Philotas of the plot. That Philotas would dismiss the story without relating it to the king seems at least reasonable. After his arrest – while admitting that he'd heard of the plot – Philotas claimed that he had not taken it seriously. Dimnus died, either during his arrest or by suicide, but before he could give evidence.

Philotas might have been unpopular with his colleagues in the army. According to Plutarch, Philotas' own father had cause to admonish him: 'Son, don't make so much of yourself.' Somewhat older than Alexander, he was given to condescending remarks that were no doubt offensive to the king – calling him 'a boy who owed his title to others' efforts!' He also apparently had a taste for luxury, but then again a generosity that exceeded his own intemperance. When a friend asked for money and Philotas' steward said there was none to give, Philotas rebuked the steward, saying, 'What do you mean – have I no plate or furniture to sell?' Philotas' mistress Antigone, whom he acquired in the spoils of battle at Issus, turned out to be one of his betrayers. Alexander instructed her to report all of his indiscretions, after Craterus had once overheard what she knew and taken her to the king.

Besides Alexander, there were other important Macedonians who had reason to look for evidence against this rival to their positions in the army. Craterus, Hephaestion and Coenus were young officers who had gained their positions under Alexander. They were not only loyal but also potentially resentful of someone like Philotas who was not unquestioning in his devotion to the king. The offensive characteristics attributed to Philotas may well have been true, but there was no concrete evidence of treachery.

Nevertheless Alexander himself demanded Philotas' death. Craterus led the outcry for torture to extract a confession

OPPOSITE Detail from the 'Alexander Sarcophagus' from Sidon, showing a warrior most often identified from his age and prominence as Parmenio.

when Philotas would not volunteer one. Under torture, he may have admitted his own guilt but he certainly did not implicate his father. The next step, however, was to have Parmenio assassinated.

This was accomplished by sending Polydamas, one of the Companions and a close friend of Philotas, with orders to the generals at Ecbatana. Not knowing what the orders contained, he was grateful to be able to serve the king when his closeness to Philotas had put his own life in jeopardy. Disguised as a nomad, the historian Curtius tells us, he travelled by dromedary and managed to cover the eight hundred miles to Ecbatana in only ten days. Speed was essential to prevent Parmenio's learning of his son's murder before his own assassination could be accomplished. Popular with the men in his command, astride Alexander's communications and holding the greater part of the Macedonian treasury, Parmenio was in a powerful position to avenge his son's death by revolting against Alexander. As usual, however, Alexander relied on the efficiency of his own undertakings. Parmenio, glad to see Polydamas, greeted his son's friend as the generals unsealed Alexander's orders and killed the old man immediately. Only then could Polydamas have realised what the orders contained and why he had been compelled to deliver them so quickly. Nothing more of Polydamas is known than this mission.

Amyntas, another friend of Philotas, was also accused of plotting against Alexander, but he pressed his defence so vigorously that he was acquitted. His two brothers were accused along with him. One of them tried to flee from prosecution but was sought out by Amyntas himself, who persuaded the brother to return and face trial. He too was acquitted. Soon thereafter Amyntas was killed in battle.

At the same time, while conspiracy was in the air, Alexander had his father's accused murderer – Alexander of Lyncestis – put to death. Of royal blood and a son-in-law of Antipater (still regent in Macedonia), this Alexander had been under arrest, travelling with the army as a prisoner for four years. The decision to kill him now, lest he be the centre of another plot against Alexander, reflects the intensity of Alexander's suspicion and fear.

Before going on, Alexander reorganised the Companion cavalry, previously under Philotas' command. Two men

In late August 330 Alexander pursued the recalcitrant Satibarzanes to Artacoana and then marched on to Drangiana. By March 329 he crossed the Hindu-Kush mountains battling against the snow and bitter cold.

were put in charge, one of them Hephaestion, who had no experience of command; and the other, Cleitus, one of Philip's old guard whose sister had nursed Alexander. The city of Phrada, where all these vicissitudes occurred, was given the name Prophthasia, meaning 'anticipation'.

Without taking winter quarters, Alexander headed north towards Bactria again. The army passed peacefully through a number of areas, one of which had been helpful to Cyrus in establishing his Persian dynasty. Alexander gave those people their independence in recognition of their contribution to the dynasty he now claimed for himself. In a departure from his continuing policy, Alexander appointed a Greek or Macedonian named Menon in place of the satrap in Arachosia. Perhaps it was because of the import- ance of the area, sitting at the foothills of the Hindu-Kush mountains, where he left four thousand mercenaries and six hundred cavalry.

Continuing north with the major body of troops, Alexander encountered the severe winter in which his men resorted

171

A silver phalera in Graeco-Bactrian style, portraying a winged griffin. A phalera is a metal dish or boss worn on a man's breast as an ornament or military emblem. The Greek influence on the art of the conquered countries was immense.

to the subterranean, snow-impacted shelters. They were also reduced to killing their own mules for food and fishing in frozen lakes. Alexander was determined to get through the mountain passes of Hindu-Kush at the earliest opportunity in order to surprise his old enemies, Bessus and Satibarzanes. Satibarzanes moved farther west in order to surround Alexander as he approached over the mountains. But Alexander, rather than let himself be diverted or surrounded, dispatched a large detachment of Companions and troops to chase the recalcitrant satrap. The chase was soon over, for Satibarzanes fell in single combat with Erigyius, another boyhood friend and Companion of Alexander's.

There remained only the conquest of Bactria and, to the north of it, Sogdiana, before heading for India. This

172

A Graeco-Bactrian silver rhyton, a drinking horn made usually of pottery or bronze, having a base in the head of a woman or animal.

seemingly simple task, involving an area no larger than Alexander had often covered in a season, took two years. It was the scene of more discord with the Macedonian army and stretched Alexander's military prowess to the limit. In the end he was to cement peace in Sogdiana only through marriage, a recourse that pays tribute to his adversaries.

The first trek through Bactria and Sogdiana was deceptively easy. Bessus had ravaged the area ahead of Alexander's troops, hoping to discourage the Macedonians without engaging them in battle. Failing to stop the advance, Bessus and his seven-thousand-strong army retreated across the Oxus river, where Alexander was prepared to follow him, using the same method of makeshift rafts that he had used so long ago on the Danube. But the satrap Spitamenes sent a

Alexander struck north for
Maracanda and the Jaxartes
(Syr-Darja). This river
marked the north-eastern
boundary of the Persian
Empire. Beyond lay the
limitless Scythian steppe
and mountains, inhabited by
wild nomadic tribesmen.

message to Alexander that if only a small force approached it would be given Bessus as a prisoner. Ptolemy was appointed by Alexander to fetch Bessus. Since Spitamenes fled at the approach of the Macedonians – though leaving Bessus naked with a wooden collar around his neck – Ptolemy was later to claim that he captured Bessus. The prisoner was tortured before being killed, a punishment for murdering Darius and claiming his throne.

Continuing north through Sogdiana, Alexander conquered the city of Maracanda (modern Samarkand) along with numerous garrisons that the Persians had built to ward off tribes from what is now the Asian Soviet republic of Kazakhskaya. He had little trouble marching through these areas, but when he summoned the Bactrian and Sogdian nobles to Bactra to consult with him, they rebelled. Again, Alexander had little trouble suppressing the uprising, except at Cyropolis, at the northern end of the province, just below the border on the Jaxartes (now the Syr-Darya) River. He overcame the city with siege machines alone. As punishment, all the men of the city were slaughtered and the women and children sold into slavery.

Meanwhile, Spitamenes, the satrap who had surrendered Bessus, took up the cause with an attack on the city of Maracanda, recently taken over by the Macedonians. Alexander did not accurately gauge the extent of the revolt and sent a small force to confront Spitamenes. Led by a Lycian interpreter named Pharnuches, the Macedonian expedition was obviously after a negotiated compromise rather than a fight. Spitamenes lost no time in routing the Macedonian forces and slaughtered them as they tried to retreat across the Zerafshan valley. It was Alexander's worst miscalculation. Though not a military decision affecting the main body of his troops, it still diminished his prestige among people who were inclined to take any sign of weakness as an encouragement to continue their resistance.

Alexander had too readily dismissed the power of his enemy for his attention was focused elsewhere: He was preoccupied with the founding of Alexandria-the-Farthest, beyond Cyropolis on the Jaxartes River. Furthermore, he was ambushed by Scythians who employed the same hit-and-run strategy that gave Spitamenes his victory. But Alexander successfully countered their advance. Leading with his javelins and archers, followed by the infantry and the

Companion cavalry, he was able to mobilise an attack that cost the Scythians one thousand dead and one hundred and fifty prisoners. The rout would have been even more severe had Alexander not contracted dysentery and been forced to return to camp on a stretcher.

Alexander had no choice but to leave his project in pursuit of Spitamenes. With half the Companion cavalry, some light-armed infantry and archers, Alexander marched one hundred and sixty miles from the Sogdian border to the Zerafshan valley in only three days, according to Arrian. Though not impossible, this prodigious speed – especially considering the relative slowness of the infantry – ranks as one of the most impressive forced marches in history. Spitamenes was again besieging Maracanda when Alexander arrived. Prepared and practised for the encounter, Alexander's army was able to cope with the guerilla-like tactics of the Bactrian forces. But Spitamenes still managed to escape with his army, so Alexander had the Zerafshan valley devastated to prevent their return.

The winter of 328 was now coming and Alexander's troops had not rested for two years. It was essential to take up winter quarters, though Spitamenes was still in troublesome revolt. It could not have been an easy time. The Macedonian army received substantial reinforcements and Alexander had to think of a way to reorganise the army to contend with his mobile, nomadic enemy.

He decided to divide the troops into five units, each with a different leader. Though these leaders in no way infringed on Alexander's overall authority, it was the first time that units of equal strength were given autonomy. During the winter Alexander received several envoys from the leaders of bordering areas. Although Sogdiana remained an annoyance, the respect and cooperation accorded him by neighbouring satraps meant he could proceed to India as soon as he had conquered Spitamenes and the Sogdian uprising.

The whole of the following spring and summer were absorbed in the pursuit of Spitamenes. The natives had been given enough time to retreat to fortifications, which had to be subdued one by one. The countryside was scoured by the five new columns acting independently. Finally Sogdiana was quieted, but Spitamenes had fled to Bactria. During this frustrating period oil was discovered bubbling out of the ground. The first time Europeans had encountered such a

The massive outer walls of
Balkh, capital of Bactria.
Alexander took winter
quarters here in 328 BC.

phenomenon, it was compared to olive oil 'though the earth was unsuited to olive trees' and was interpreted by Aristander of Telmessus as a sign of the need for hard work which would eventually be well rewarded. At one point Spitamenes seemed surrounded, as Craterus, Coenus and Alexander all pursued him across the deserts towards Bactria. Craterus' men managed to kill 150 of the elusive enemy, but Spitamenes escaped once again.

By autumn Alexander was in Maracanda with his men, reassembled for a well-deserved rest. Winter quarters that year were at Nautaca, but during the autumn there was a break for athletic contests and some carousing. With Spitamenes apparently no more manageable than he had been the whole previous year, the relaxation was more a sign of weariness than of optimism. The military problems only exacerbated the tensions caused by the continuing conflict between European and Asian subjects in Alexander's camp.

At one evening's festivities Alexander and Cleitus started a verbal slanging match. Cleitus, it seems, was upset at a song with verses that insulted Macedonian leaders defeated in recent battles against Spitamenes. Cleitus considered the song to be in especially bad taste considering that it was being sung in front of both Macedonians and Persians.

'And Macedonians should not be insulted in front of enemies and barbarians,' said Cleitus, a man with a quick temper.

Alexander replied tauntingly, 'If you are disguising cowardice as misfortune, then you must be talking about yourself.'

Cleitus sprang to his feet and shouted, 'Yes, my cowardice saved your life, you who call yourself the son of gods. It was the blood of these Macedonians who made you great and now you disown your own father and call yourself the son of Ammon.'

'You scum,' shouted Alexander. 'You expect to stir up the Macedonians and not pay for it!'

'But we do pay for it,' Cleitus retorted. 'Just think of our rewards for the effort we give you. It is the dead who are happy, for they are not beaten with Persian rods and forced to beg Persians for an audience with their own king.'

Still in control of himself, Alexander turned to others at the table and said mockingly of Cleitus, 'When you see the

179

Greeks walking about among the Macedonians, don't they look like demigods among wild beasts?'

Cleitus would not desist and shouted to Alexander, 'Speak out what you have to say – or don't invite free men to dine with you. Perhaps you would prefer to be alone with your barbarians and slaves who will prostrate themselves before your white tunic and Persian girdle.'

Alexander now lost control of himself. He threw an apple at Cleitus, then reached for his dagger. A bodyguard had prudently removed it already, but rather than calm the proceedings, it alarmed Alexander. He ordered his trumpeter to call the troops, but he refused and Alexander attacked him. The king screamed in Macedonian for his bodyguards, the vernacular being a sure sign of his distress.

Cleitus would still not be calmed; so his friends pushed him from the room. When he stormed back in, it was with a cry from Euripides' play *Andromache*: 'Alas, what evil custom reigns in Greece.'

Alexander grabbed a bodyguard's spear and ran Cleitus through, killing him instantly. His immediate reaction was to spear himself through the neck, but he was restrained and

Seleucus I portrayed here on the obverse of one of his own tetradrachms. He had married the daughter of the rebel Spitamenes and later succeeded Alexander as king of Asia.

dragged to his quarters, where he 'sobbed in an agony of remorse', according to Plutarch. The whole of this account comes from Plutarch; certain discrepancies occur with other historians, like the question of whether Cleitus left the banqueting hall before he was killed. But there is little question that the killing was an accident.

Plutarch says that Alexander was consoled only by the reminder from Aristander that the king had had a dream foretelling these events. The dream showed Cleitus dressed in black with Parmenio and his sons – hardly a comfort to the king, one would think, but it did at least assure him that events were preordained.

It was in a highly charged atmosphere that Alexander accidentally killed Cleitus, the man who led half the Companion cavalry and had – as Cleitus insisted on reminding him – saved Alexander's life at the battle of Granicus. The killing, accidental as it was, served to warn the Macedonian army of Alexander's determination to have his way. And it further ensured his power by eliminating one more noble. When Alexander retreated to his quarters for three days, he also – purposely or not – warned his troops that without his leadership they were left at the farthest bounds of the known world, having no way back. No doubt an incident that greatly disturbed Alexander, he was nevertheless capable of turning it to his advantage, showing again that his limitations and capacities as an authoritative leader were insolubly linked.

Spitamenes now decided on a pitched battle, having been joined by three thousand men from a fierce northern tribe, the Massagetae. In the battle the original force of Bactrians and Sogdians surrendered after fifteen hundred of their cavalry were killed, but Spitamenes fled with the Massagetae. When they heard that Alexander was prepared to chase them, they cut off Spitamenes' head and offered it to Alexander. It was not quite the end of his valiant career, though, for Spitamenes' family were captured by Alexander, who accorded them royal treatment. Four years later Spitamenes' daughter married Seleucus, the general who founded the greatest of Alexander's successor states.

It was with much more optimism that Alexander took up winter quarters in Nautaca. For the moment the Sogdian revolt appeared to be finished and India could be approached

Detail from a felt wall hanging
from the tomb of a chieftain at Pazyryk.
A Scythian warrior on horseback
faces his king or satrap who is seated on
a throne in the Iranian style.

at the beginning of the next campaign. At this propitious time Alexander dared introduce the practice of *proskynesis*, which was an accepted Persian custom of prostrating oneself before the king. Though it did not specifically entail considering the king as a god, it certainly broke with Greek custom in which only the gods were bowed to. The growing anomalies of a court divided by opposing customs and traditions were intended by Alexander to be reconciled with everyone performing *proskynesis*.

The notion of 'fusing' the two elements of Alexander's camp was not just a gesture towards reconciliation. It definitely required a complete reorientation of the Greek and Macedonian perspective on royalty, a change that Cleitus' death warned could not easily be achieved. The adaptation was to take place gradually. Hephaestion selected a small number of Macedonians, Greeks and Persians to perform *proskynesis* at a given ceremony. To these men he probably explained its limited meaning, conveying that it was no more demeaning an act than any subject performed for any king; it was merely a different form of address.

At the given time, Alexander handed a cup of wine to one of the chosen people, who offered a libation at the altar and prostrated himself before the king. Alexander then kissed him and the ceremony proceeded without incident from man to man until it was Callisthenes' turn. He refused to bow to the king, an act of defiance the king did not at first notice. When it was brought to his attention, Alexander refused the kiss to Callisthenes, to which the court historian retorted, 'Then I shall be poorer by a kiss.'

That remark, which stunned the king and gathered assembly, ended the attempt to force any Greek or Macedonian to perform *proskynesis*. No doubt Alexander harboured a lingering grudge against Callisthenes, for while the Asian subjects continued to perform it before the king, he had Callisthenes to thank for its being ridiculed by the Greeks and Macedonians. It was likely, moreover, that Callisthenes had told Hephaestion he would perform the ceremony and then refused to do so when the time came.

Alexander soon had his revenge. During a speech in praise of the Macedonians, Callisthenes was goaded by the king into damning the Macedonians since, said Alexander, quoting from Euripides, 'On noble subjects all men can speak well.' Callisthenes took up the challenge with alacrity and said

183

how much Philip, Alexander's father, was aided in his conquest of Greece by the dissension among the states. He added a quotation to the effect that in times of trouble the greatest villains get the upper hand. Since he was a Greek, Callisthenes was then accused of betraying his actual feelings. And so this pathetic figure, who had done his best to promote Alexander's journey – to the point of calling him a god – was himself betrayed. When Alexander had him accused of an assassination plot the following year, he had few defenders.

Though Spitamenes was dead, there were still pockets of resistance in Sogdiana. Leaders who had fled from Alexander were now holed up in mountain retreats, practically inaccessible and certainly impervious to attack. The first of these mountain fortresses was the 'Sogdian rock' where Alexander's future father-in-law Oxyartes felt he had no reason to fear the Macedonians. The defending forces hurled insults and mockery at Alexander's men, calling down to them that they would need winged soldiers to reach their refuge. Alexander got three hundred mountain-climbing volunteers (thirty of whom fell to their deaths in the attempt) to use ropes and tent pegs to scale the mountain. They accomplished the feat in one night, so that Alexander's herald could call up the next day that the defenders should 'look up to see the king's airborne soldiers'.

Oxyartes surrendered at this point and helped Alexander in his subsequent attacks. At the next stronghold Alexander asked whether the leader was a fighting man. When Oxyartes said no, Alexander made the telling remark, 'Then it doesn't matter what his defences are like.' In fact Oxyartes was summoned to consult with the Sogdian forces and they surrendered without a fight. The alliance contracted with Oxyartes through his daughter Roxane was a political move on Alexander's part. It soothed the Sogdians so Alexander could move on to India. However alluring Roxane was made to sound in legend, she must not yet have reached puberty, for she did not have a child for four years after her marriage to Alexander.

Now in the spring of 327, Alexander was finally prepared to go into India, but one more unfortunate event was to come first. A conspiracy of Royal Pages was discovered, its aim being to kill Alexander. Feelings had been aroused when

Alexander had a page whipped for interfering with a hunting party of the king's. The page presumed to take a shot before the king and was appropriately punished, but a number of pages – at least nine who are known – were prepared to conspire in an assassination attempt. Because Callisthenes was the boys' master and, more important, had aroused the king's enmity, he was accused with them. The pages were executed and Callisthenes was held prisoner for two years while his physical state deteriorated. He finally died, a prisoner of the expedition whose exploits he had been employed to extol.

8 To India

and Back

HAD ALEXANDER BEEN a fictional character his creator could have done no better than lose his subject in the wilds of India, fighting armies on elephants and encountering peoples, both savage and civilised, who had never been seen by Europeans before. That the historical Alexander actually did have such an experience has naturally been made much of in the romances. For a fictional character, it might have sufficed to let him go off into the unknown, never to return. For the real hero of history, it is appropriate that he did return, having conquered peoples as far as he went and come back by routes that exercised his troops to the limit of their endurance and imagination.

Alexander himself took the main body of his men through the unbearable desert of Gedrosia while Nearchus, a boyhood friend and Companion, was allowed to take the sea voyage with its spectacular sights. It is difficult to know how much Alexander knew about India before he set out. There was almost no information of any accuracy available in Greece or Macedonia. But Alexander did receive envoys from various potentates, he had some scouting reports and the Persian archives possibly yielded some useful information. Alexander knew enough to be able to play one leader off against another, allowing him to concentrate his efforts on one great confrontation with Porus.

The campaign to India began in the late spring of 327. There were some preliminary affairs to attend to, establishing the Macedonian Amyntas as satrap in the particularly strategic area of Bactria and replacing the garrison commander at one of the Alexandrias on grounds of incompetence. Before he had got to the Khyber Pass he was met by several Indian leaders, whom he had summoned. One of them was Taxiles, who ruled the area beyond the Indus river and the accord established between the two leaders would assure Alexander's conquests hundreds of miles beyond the boundaries of the Persian Empire – assuming he got to the Indus.

Reaching the Indus entailed several hard campaigns against tribes Alexander sought out. Half of the Macedonian army went through the Khyber Pass with the baggage and entourage, but Alexander took the other half on a northward detour where he encountered fierce native forces. One of the battles resulted in the capture of forty thousand Indians and two hundred and fifty thousand cattle. The best of the

PREVIOUS PAGES Near the top of the Khyber Pass leading to Afghanistan.

OPPOSITE While half the Macedonian army went through the Khyber Pass, Alexander, with Craterus as his second in command, planned to take a mobile column through the hill country of Bajaur and Swat (right). Here Alexander faced some of the toughest and bloodiest encounters in his campaign.

188

captured cattle Alexander had transported back to Macedonia to improve native stock. He was slightly wounded in one battle, and in another, after securing the surrender of the enemy forces, he had them slaughtered. Implausible excuses have been given for such viciousness, but enough of Alexander's growing wilfulness and instinctive distrust had been demonstrated to make them equally sufficient reasons.

In this same mountainous area before the Khyber Pass and India, Alexander came upon a colony of people descended from Europeans. Because vines grew in the area, which was known as Nysa, their god Shiva was associated with Dionysus, a relationship Alexander encouraged. The Greek patheon was dedicated to gods with human traits, whose prowess was reflected on earth both through the myths of their accomplishments and through the achievements of mortals whom they favoured. Since Alexander was to travel beyond Nysa, and so cover territory which was unknown even to Dionysus, association with the gods was natural. A cult of Alexander consequently grew throughout the Indian campaign. There is still uncertainty about just who these people at Nysa were, but Alexander was quick to take advantage of the situation and he left them to govern themselves, unfettered by a new satrap.

Though Alexander now had access to the Indus, he would not cross it until he conquered all the natives who had taken refuge in a mountain retreat seven thousand feet high with a commanding view of the river. Next to it was an even higher peak, which – according to native guides – gave best access to the 'rock' (identified early in this century by Sir Aurel Stein as Pīr-sar). Ptolemy took some hand-picked troops up the larger, adjoining peak, but Alexander was forced to retreat when he tried to follow the next day. The king then sent a secret message to Ptolemy to coordinate the attack so that Alexander and his men were covered when they made the ascent on the following day.

There still remained the problem of bridging the gap between peaks. Under heavy attack, Alexander had his men start a causeway, which soon supported siege machines and discouraged further attack as it was built. In three days it was finished, a feat that shocked the Indians into capitulation. The defenders had intended to escape during the night, but Alexander heard of the plan and rushed the fortress; he left a native in charge while he marched north.

Bronze crater from Dherveni in Macedonia, late fourth century BC. Dionysus, god of wine, rests in the lap of Ariadne. It was said that Dionysus reached India; after imposing his worship he returned to Greece in a chariot drawn by leopards.

Hephaestion meanwhile was sent down river to build a bridge across it. Alexander soon joined him, having sailed sixteen miles in hastily constructed boats. Across the Indus, Taxiles greeted Alexander with seven hundred cavalry and many gifts as tribute. Taxiles' voluntary submission enabled him to abandon his feuds with neighbouring states, which Alexander took over for him. The Macedonian forces marched north to Taxiles' capital, twenty miles north-west of present-day Rawalpindi. Alexander promised his ally as much territory as he wanted.

The capital, Taxila, was a great crossroads market place where Alexander's army came upon a mud-brick maze of Hindu street life. Poor men unable to pay a dowry sold their eligible daughters at auction. The rich dyed their beards snow white, blue, red, purple and green. They wore linen tunics, capes and turbans wound round their heads. Those who could afford them carried parasols and had high leather shoes. The streets teemed with nomads, peasants and traders. There were ascetics and wise men who blessed passers-by by putting oil on their foreheads.

Alexander sent one of the steersmen of the Greek fleet, Onesicritus, to search out a group of ascetics known as Gymnosophists. A former student of Diogenes, the envoy had to go no farther than two miles from Taxila to find a group of the naked wise men, who asked Onesicritus to take his clothes off. Embarrassed, he excused himself because of the heat and was allowed to talk to the wise men through three interpreters. But the subjects of conversation were somewhat confined, according to one of the seers, because using interpreters 'is like asking pure water to flow through mud'. Nevertheless, the leading wise man expressed admiration of Alexander – 'the only philosopher in armour he had ever heard of' – while commenting that Socrates, Pythagoras and Diogenes 'were decent men who paid too much attention to convention and not enough to nature'. Two of the wise men were persuaded to join Alexander for a meal, during which the younger one entertained the Europeans by standing on one leg the night through, holding a five-foot beam all the while. The older seer, called Canalus in Greek, accepted the invitation to join Alexander's army because he had already served his thirty-seven-year stint of asceticism and was allowed to alter his way of life. Canalus' death was to cause a sensation among

Artifacts from Taxila:
ABOVE a necklace.
RIGHT an earring.

A silver decadrachm, struck at Babylon to commemorate the victory of the Jhelum. It shows Alexander on Bucephalus, attacking Porus' war elephant with his lance.

OPPOSITE The introduction of elephants to areas further west resulted from this campaign. Sometimes the elephants were equipped with towers for transporting soldiers. This elephant painted on a clay dish of Italian workmanship, early third century BC, is one that Pyrrhus, king of Epirus, brought to Italy.

Alexander's troops when he demanded that he be allowed to die on a funeral pyre rather than continue as an invalid.

The great Indian battle was approaching against Taxiles' major enemy, Porus. A shrewd strategist armed with a large force and elephants, Porus made an imposing adversary, especially for Alexander's army which had never encountered elephants in battle before. Though the beasts would seem to be a slow and immobile encumbrance, they had a regal splendour that infused Indian mythology and soon became adapted to the West. Alexander's funeral bier was decorated with elephant heads, and coins made to commemorate the king after his death showed his head adorned with elephant skins, whether or not (and probably not) he ever wore them.

At this first battle the elephants were able to prevent Alexander crossing the Jhelum River, where Porus' troops were massed, simply by frightening the Macedonian horses. Porus had enough elephants to cover the whole area where Alexander considered crossing. Crossing the Jhelum River, therefore, was considered one of the great military feats of ancient history. Hannibal seems to have used the same stratagem on the Rhône and the whole manoeuvre demonstrates unquestionably the ability of Alexander to handle any military situation. The last of his major battles, it made a fitting climax to his career.

On the eastern bank of the Jhelum, Porus had some thirty to fifty thousand infantry, a thousand chariots and between eighty-five and two hundred elephants. Alexander had heard that his crossing would be resisted and so ordered Coenus, still with the fleet from the previous crossing, to have the boats cut in half to be transported to the Jhelum. Alexander embarked on a highly successful diversionary

manoeuvre by having his men make daily marches up and down the river as though looking for a place to cross. Divided into five groups, these forces kept Porus' men on the other side on constant alert. This took up some weeks, and in the end Porus discontinued his close supervision of Alexander's activities, allowing his scouts to keep an eye on Alexander instead. In order to deceive the enemy still further, Alexander had corn brought to his camp, as though he expected to remain where he was for some time.

Since this was the spring rainy season, it was reasonable that Alexander would remain on the western shore until at least midsummer. But to Alexander the rain held the advantage of concealing his movements. So he proceeded with his attack once he was assured that Porus had discounted the possibility. He divided his army into thirds, with himself leading the forward group of about five thousand cavalry and ten thousand infantry. The rearguard remained at the camp, with instructions to cross the river if Porus took all of his troops to meet Alexander's crossing. Otherwise they were to stay put. The second group followed Alexander up the western shore of the Jhelum and stationed itself at various fords with instructions to follow across once Alexander had made contact with the enemy. Alexander's group marched seventeen miles upstream, staying far enough from shore not to be seen by Porus' guards, aided by the blanket of torrential rain that further concealed their activities.

The operation began at dusk and by the middle of the night Alexander had crossed to a large island in the middle of the Jhelum. By then the force was seen and Porus sent his son with a contingent of two thousand cavalry and one hundred and twenty chariots to meet Alexander's troops on arrival; but Alexander had not realised that he was not on the other shore, and had to find another crossing place. A safe crossing was a remarkable feat and it was accomplished in a very short time. Once across, they engaged in battle almost immediately, with the horse-archers in the lead to cover while Alexander drew up his order of battle. Not knowing the strength of the Indian troops, he at first proceeded with a defensive manoeuvre, but then switched to an attack, in which Porus' son died and four hundred of the Indian cavalry were slaughtered. The chariots were driven into a claybank and captured.

Porus' son was no match for
the best cavalry units in
the whole Macedonian army
and Alexander's genius as
a field commander.

The major battle was still to be fought. Porus had wisely kept back to prevent being encircled by Alexander's rearguard. But now, in this crucial period, he did not come forward but gave Alexander the chance to regroup his men after the first encounter with the Indian contingent. Finally he moved his major force upstream towards Alexander's landing, looking for suitably hard and level ground to await the Macedonian advance. He left a small force behind to protect his rear, as Alexander brought his forces down the east side of the river.

Porus' battle line was formidable, but it lacked flexibility. He had some twenty thousand infantry, two thousand cavalry and the elephants, drawn in one long line with the cavalry on the wings and the elephants at intervals of about a hundred feet, which covered most of the infantry standing behind them. Alexander's strategy was to take advantage of their inflexibility by drawing an attack in one direction and then having another attack to put the enemy off balance. This he accomplished by concentrating most of the cavalry under his command on the right wing. With a force of at least four thousand cavalry plus a thousand mounted archers in the lead, he drew Porus' forces into a full-scale attack on this end. At the same time Coenus took two cavalry regiments round to the rear of the Indian force, where they attacked a surprised and diverted enemy. The Indians' elephants, now hemmed in, began to panic and cause more damage to their own side than to Alexander's. Only at this point did the Macedonian infantry enter the battle.

They completed the rout, though Porus himself refused to surrender or flee. Wounded and tired, he finally acceded to the plea of a former ally to give himself up to Alexander. Asked by Alexander what he would request of the conqueror, Porus answered, 'To be treated like a king.' Alexander of course granted the request, for he needed Porus as an ally – and was always glad to reward bravery and chivalry. Porus and his neighbour Taxiles were now able to keep an eye on each other, for though they were both allies of Alexander, there is no reason to believe that their own enmity had subsided. Alexander even gave more land to Porus to equalise his position with Taxiles', though one had always been an ally and the other a recent enemy.

As a result of the battle, Alexander's great horse

Bucephalus died. He either dropped dead from exhaustion or was wounded. The battle had taken its toll on all the animals, for Alexander had had the elephants attacked on the trunk, their most vulnerable spot, with scythe-like weapons. Alexander led a procession of mourning for the horse and gave the name Bucephela to one of the two cities built on the battle site. Craterus, who was left to oversee the building of the cities, was also instructed to build a fleet. Whether from natural curiosity, or a real belief that the presence of crocodiles and Egyptian beans indicated (wrongly) that the Jhelum was a headwater of the Nile, Alexander was determined to send an exploratory expedition down the river.

For the moment, however, he continued his journey eastward, where he had some trouble with recalcitrant tribes, notably the Cathaeans, whose city took days and thousands of lives on both sides to subdue. It was, however, Alexander's own troops who mounted the ultimate resistance to their king. At the Boas River, Alexander's empire reached its farthest limit because the soldiers would no longer follow him.

Whether he knew that his destination at the 'Eastern Ocean' was still twelve hundred miles away is impossible to guess. It was already hundreds of miles farther than Aristotle had believed when asserting that the ocean could be seen from the summit of Hindu-Kush. If Alexander, as is likely, had learned that there was a Ganges River after the Boas and Jhelum, then he must have realised that his destination was still a long way off.

From what *it* learned, the army camp seethed with discontent. The midsummer monsoon had dampened spirits which were already affected by rumours of the lands beyond – populated by superhuman men and kings with innumerable elephants of even greater size than those just encountered. Morale had been sustained for such a long time that Alexander might well have assumed that his troops shared his own indomitable adventuring spirit, but looking back, we wonder rather at how it managed to last so long. Coenus took up the cause of the soldiers and told Alexander in a conciliatory but firm speech, 'Do not lead us against our will, for we cannot show the same determination if we lack enthusiasm.'

Alexander retired to his tent for three days, giving his troops the chance to reconsider. As happened when Alexander killed Cleitus, the king's isolation might rally the troops in support of him, not least because they would realise the danger of being left in the wilderness without their king. But they were unmoved by threats or cajolery and in the end Alexander had to decide to turn back. There is no doubt that Alexander would have preferred to go farther. He had with him his full complement of troops, along with five thousand of Porus' Indians and all of his elephants. Another five thousand cavalry and seven thousand infantry had just arrived from Greece as reinforcements.

Though it had never happened before, Alexander knew when he was beaten. He had priests and seers offer sacrifices, but as expected, the omens did not favour a crossing. This face-saving ceremony relieved the troops and reconciled Alexander to them. Twelve huge towers facing east were built to the gods. According to legend, but not as yet confirmed by archaeologists, Alexander also had a huge camp staked out, with tents and beds to fit men eight-foot tall. This camp, surrounded by a fifty-foot ditch, would intimidate any eastern conqueror who intended to encroach on Alexander's territory.

Camp was broken and the army headed back to the Jhelum, where Craterus was having the fleet built. There was still one further campaign of Alexander's to subdue tribes along the rivers he was following. There were more adventures and ordeals to undergo, but Alexander had seen the end of his major ambition. At the very end of his life he was planning an expedition in Arabia. He made changes in the organisation of his empire, but these developments were left in a rudimentary state. It was the impulse to continue his conquests that motivated the man. This first and last disappointment heralded the end of the great campaign and for Alexander this meant finding substitute ambitions.

Before the army reached the Jhelum River, Coenus, the general who had led the defiance of Alexander, died. No details of his death are recorded, except for an historian's terse comment that 'he died of illness and was buried with all the magnificence that circumstances allowed'. The possibility that he was deliberately removed cannot be discounted, despite the meagre evidence, for not only had he stood up to Alexander but he also must have gained much support from the troops in whose interest he spoke. With his death

A head of Alexander found
in Alexandria, Egypt.

Alexander could no doubt face the future with greater
equanimity.

He managed to channel his disappointment into organising his river voyage. Eight hundred ships were prepared
in the space of two months. When the fleet set sail in
November 325, the crews consisted of Phoenicians, Cypriots,
Carians and Egyptians while the passengers were the select
group of bodyguards, Companions, archers and Agrianians.
The rest of the army was divided between Craterus on the
west bank and Hephaestion on the east. The expedition
had not gone far when it encountered the Mallians, a fierce
and warring nation.

So Alexander disembarked for his last major campaign,
which followed an elaborate plan devised to use all the
separate troops in their different locations. Alexander took

his group through a desert to the west of Malli and then pursued the unsuspecting enemy towards the other troops still by the river. It was a successful strategy which caught the Mallians by surprise. Alexander and his troops indulged in wanton slaughter and destruction during the campaign. But the troops showed a marked reluctance to fight. In the words of Curtius, an historian with no love of Alexander: 'The Macedonians believed that they had already encountered every danger. When they knew that a fresh war with the most warlike nations of India still remained, they were struck with sudden fear and began again to upbraid the king with mutinous mutterings.'

Alexander had to lead the assault on the major Mallian stronghold after the troops refused to storm the walls without him. They did follow him over the wall and killed five thousand Mallians while many of the others died in the fires they had set themselves in an attempt to prevent Alexander from capturing them. The remaining Mallians regrouped across the river, holding another fortress. Here again Alexander had to lead his forces over the wall. This

A detail from the 'Alexander Sarcophagus' thought to represent Hephaestion.

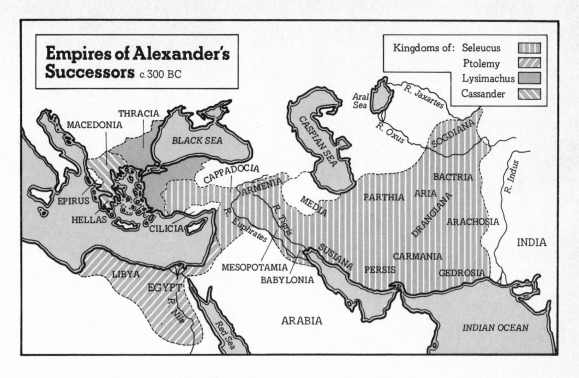

Empires of Alexander's Successors c.300 BC

Kingdoms of: Seleucus
Ptolemy
Lysimachus
Cassander

time, however, he was left abandoned on the parapets, perhaps because the ladders broke under the weight of those following him. Alexander jumped inside the city and started beating off his attackers while his followers clambered over to get to him. The first one over was killed almost immediately. Then Alexander was struck in the chest by an arrow that pierced his breastplate. He was immediately put under the protection of Peucestas bearing Achilles' sacred shield of Ilium. He was surrounded by his men until he could be safely removed, the Macedonian troops meanwhile overwhelming the last of the Mallian defences. Thousands more were slaughtered.

Alexander was treated for the puncture of his lung, but a rumour reached the troops farther down the river that the king had already died. Alexander thought it best to sail down river as soon as possible, lest his injury cause even worse trouble for the army in its low state of morale. Arrian tells the moving story of Alexander being borne towards his men, the parasol protecting him being lifted so the men could see him. At first all they perceived was a corpse but as soon as Alexander waved his arm 'so unexpected was the sense of relief that many, in spite of themselves, burst into tears.'

The Jhelum River feeds into the Indus along its extended course. As the army moved down river, it encountered more resistance but now Alexander had the full support of his appreciative army. Despite their facing an enemy aroused to fight a religious crusade, passage down the Indus was successfully secured. On the way down, Alexander designated two Alexandrias to be built, evidence that he intended to encourage trade by land and sea between East and West.

The mouths of the Indus formed a delta in a configuration that no longer exists. Alexander first sailed the western side from the city of Pattala, only to find it beset by tides, which were unfamiliar to the Greeks. Several boats were lost and he returned to the city in order to attempt the eastern side, which proved to be more placid. Nearchus, who had been admiral of the fleet down the Jhelum and Indus, begged Alexander to allow him to continue leading the fleet for the projected exploratory journey to the Persian Gulf. Alexander was reluctant, not because of the dangers of the sailing itself but because of the unreliability of supplies and food along the route. He did however relent to Nearchus' importuning.

Alexander himself was intending to cross the Gedrosian desert, a project so dangerous and foolhardy that historians have been hard put to explain it. Reasons advanced include Alexander's determination to punish his troops for their mutiny or to prove that despite turning back and his wounds received in the recent campaign, he was still invincible. In any event, the journey took sixty gruelling days, with the temperature at 127° during the day. Though the army was expecting to travel only by night, it was sometimes necessary to bear the midday heat in order to reach the next watering hole. The troops were reduced to eating their own pack mules. Trickles of water hardly sufficient for the thirsty army turned overnight into raging torrents and many soldiers drowned in the unforeseen – and unpredictable – exigencies. Guides lost their way in the trackless desert and baggage trains had to be abandoned. Soldiers who fell behind never caught up again. Three-quarters of the troops who made the journey died along the way, making for yet another humiliation for Alexander. His leadership at least is honoured with one story. When he was offered a helmet full of water he tipped it in the sand because his troops could not share it.

Until his own situation became desperate, Alexander was

even sending supplies to the coast to be sure that Nearchus and the fleet had enough. The worry over Nearchus was unnecessary, for the admiral soon came to Alexandria (Gulashkird) in Carmania to reassure the king and recount his incredible findings. Stone-age tribes, described as Fish Eaters, lived by the shore in whalebone huts. Even their few sheep tasted of fish, which they ate raw. Here Nearchus would not let his crew go ashore; their privation was so severe that he feared their attempting to escape. At an island sacred to the Sun, on the other hand, he forced his men to land in order to disprove the local legend that men disappeared on the island. They ran across a school of whales, whose shooting spouts frightened the men. Nearchus had bugles trumpeted to scare them away, which it did. Though reassured, Alexander was still reluctant to let Nearchus continue the journey to Susa, but again he relented and Nearchus rejoined his fleet.

Alexander had other preoccupations, which began at Pura, once he had made the desert crossing. Now that he was coming back into lands he had already conquered, he had to deal with the governors he had left in charge. It was over four years since he had passed the Hindu-Kush into Bactria. In that time, the satraps and European financial officers had been able to act without restraint. Their excesses were not in themselves so serious as much as in the potential threat they posed to Alexander. Cleomenes, who had by now taken control of Egypt, had exceeded his authority as much as the men Alexander was to punish, but the king did not challenge Cleomenes. In fact, in a letter assumed to be authentic, Alexander promised to excuse him without reservation if he would build some shrines to Hephaestion, who died soon after this stop in Pura.

Alexander was met by numerous officials from all parts of the empire when he emerged from the desert. They had been instructed to bring supplies and reinforcements, in response to which the Persian satrap in Parthia, for instance, sent cooked food delivered by his two sons. It is notable that this satrap was one of the few Asians to keep his post in the succeeding months. Macedonian and Thracian generals whom Alexander had sent to Ecbatana arrived with six thousand troops. Among the generals was the brother of Coenus as well as the men who had been ordered six years before to kill Parmenio. There was common gossip,

205

reported to Alexander, that these men had pillaged the city, stealing precious jewels and ornaments from the temples, living in debauchery and making free with their authority.

Alexander had them tried for abusing their positions, for which they were condemned and two of them, including Coenus' brother, executed. The third was held under arrest and the fate of the fourth is unknown, but six hundred of his followers were executed, so his death can also be assumed. The real reasons for their deaths involve a complexity of issues, all of which may have influenced the king. Their killing of Parmenio may have put Alexander too much in their debt or worried him about his own safety. Curtius adds the possibility that they had solicitously expressed concern for the king's welfare, which he interpreted as a slight to his invincibility.

Alexander was not turning bloodthirsty for its own murderous sake. Other executions were to follow, but they all had some political motive. No doubt he felt less compunction than ever before about nipping opposition in the bud. He perhaps had more imaginary – as well as justifiable – fears than in the past, for the power centres of his empire no longer rested merely within the Macedonian army and in proximity to the king. They were spread among all the satraps and generals who had troops and money at their command.

Further severe measures were taken in Carmania. Alexander executed the satrap on the grounds that he had been planning a revolt. It has also been suggested that he was looking for a scapegoat for the disaster in the Gedrosian desert, blaming the satrap for providing insufficient supplies. In his place was put a Macedonian who had not otherwise been heard of. Having an obscure figure in this position, which was soon extended to cover Gedrosia as well, indicates Alexander's desire to augment his power by using people completely dependent on his favour.

It was an easy march from Carmania to Persis, but Alexander had Hephaestion take the greater part of the troops along the shore, where the weather was milder and the supplies more readily available. On his way overland with the Companions and select troops, Alexander came upon Cyrus' tomb. They stopped to pay their respects, for Alexander claimed to be the legitimate successor of the Achaemenid dynasty, founded by Cyrus. On close inspection they found that the tomb had been vandalised. The

The tomb of Cyrus the Great at Pasargadae.
Onesicritus, who inspected it with
Alexander, reported that its inscription,
in Greek and Persian, read simply:
'Here lie I, Cyrus, King of Kings.'

guardian Magi were tortured to extract a confession or information. None was forthcoming, and so the investigation ended.

When Alexander got to Pasargadae, however, the acting satrap, a rich Persian names Orxines, was accused of and executed for the looting. He had taken the place of the appointed satrap who had died, and there is no reason to assume that Alexander took offence at this smooth transition of power. A reasonable explanation for the execution comes from Curtius, who claims that Alexander's favoured eunuch Bagoas cooked up the plot to get rid of Orxines. He got others to accuse the satrap of the looting because Orxines had not given anything – meaning wealth – to the eunuch. In Orxines' place, Alexander appointed Peucestas, the man who had saved his life with the sacred shield fighting the Mallians. Though a Macedonian, Peucestas adopted Persian dress and learned the Persian language, acts of conciliation that pleased Alexander but displeased the rest of the Macedonians.

In this atmosphere, personal danger facing Alexander's officials led Harpalus, his lifelong friend and Companion, to flee to Greece. Harpalus had lived in Babylon in splendid debauchery, importing Greek mistresses and taking full advantage of his position. He had fled to Greece once before, in 333, but now he believed he would be shown no mercy by Alexander, though he had been excused the first time. So with six thousand mercenaries and five thousand talents he left. After killing the generals from Ecbatana, Alexander had demanded that the satraps dismiss all their mercenaries, an act that would have left bands of soldiers roaming in Asia, rendering officials like Harpalus defenceless. Rather than disband them, Harpalus led them back to Athens, where he could expect to be welcomed, for he had been made a citizen there after helping the city during their famine in 330.

Towards the end of February 324, Alexander reached Susa with Nearchus and the fleet not far behind. Alexander arranged games and sacrifices to celebrate the successful completion of the voyage. A splendid celebration was organised, with Alexander distributing gold crowns to his leaders and notable soldiers. This marked the end of the Indian campaign, but even this celebration paled in comparison with the five-day feast that was soon to follow.

A tent was built for Alexander, half a mile in circumference and supported on thirty-foot columns studded with precious stones and metals. There were gold curtains, expensive carpets and a hundred couches put inside. Entertainment came from India and the West, with varieties of music, conjurors and actors. The climax of the celebration was the marriage of ninety leading Macedonians and Greeks to Persian women. Alexander married his second wife Barsine, Darius' daughter, and Hephaestion married her sister, so that – according to Alexander's wishes – his children would be cousins of Hephaestion's.

It might appear that Alexander was successfully embarking on the important and far-reaching goal of forging a new cross-cultural society. This wedding has been pointed to as the culmination of Alexander's achievement, which would have gone further had he lived longer. In fact, nothing was so evident as the continued dissension he faced. In Susa he killed the satrap and his son on charges of maladministration. Like all his appointments to satrapies, a European – in this case a Macedonian – replaced a

The forty years following Alexander's death saw a savage and ruthless struggle between his surviving marshals.
ABOVE Coin of Cassander, Alexander's successor in Macedonia, who had Roxane and her thirteen-year-old son killed; Alexander's direct line became extinct.
LEFT An idealised bust of Ptolemy who is usually seen as hook-nosed and prognathous. He succeeded Alexander in Egypt.

Persian. With one notable exception, the marriages to Persian women were abandoned as soon as Alexander died. This union by blood can more plausibly be considered an attempt to forge by personal ties what political ones had failed to achieve. Alexander's entire relationship with Greece and the West had been ignored until now, and what little he had recently been exposed to augured ill for his intentions and hopes.

At the time of the mass marriages Alexander handsomely rewarded all of his men who had taken Asian women and legitimised their marriages. The money he gave them was less an extension of his policy than a means of placating the troops, who were again being mutinous. He also asked the soldiers to submit an accounting of their debts in order to pay them as a reward. Suspicious that Alexander would punish the profligate, they had to be reassured that the king's motives were not sinister. When thirty thousand Persian boys who had been trained under Alexander's instructions since 327 were introduced to the court in Susa, an outcry arose against them. They had been well trained as Macedonian soldiers, but their very skill and discipline confirmed to the onlooking soldiers that Alexander intended to adopt a purely servile Persian fighting force. Alexander called them his 'successors'; the Macedonians called them 'war-dancers'. As though this were not enough, Alexander also introduced more Persians into his Companion cavalry, a move that was partly justified by the losses in the Gedrosian desert. Still, the army took offence at this and the accompanying reorganisation that gave the Persians a more prominent place.

He next offended the Greeks by having his new Exiles Decree read out at the Olympic games in 324. Though as hegemon of the Corinthian League Alexander could not make demands on the states' internal policies, the decree did have the force of compulsion. Twenty thousand exiles gathered at Olympia to hear Alexander's wish that political exiles be allowed to return to their home states. Since most states were ruled by oligarchies sympathetic to Alexander, the dissension such an act would bring about hardly suited Alexander's own interest. It is possible that he was trying to ingratiate himself again with Greeks or he might have been afraid that Harpalus would be able to recruit among the exiled bands of mercenaries. The policy was not carried out by the time of Alexander's death. Neither was his instruction that religious cults to himself be established in Greece. This order was greeted with some ridicule, a Laconian making a typically laconic remark: 'If Alexander wants to be a god, let him.' This too, though, offended the Greeks, who had never shown much love for Alexander anyway.

If the Exiles Decree had been intended to counter Harpalus, it was unnecessary. When he arrived in Athens he was not admitted to the city. He then left most of his troops and money and came back, only to be put under open arrest in the city; his seven hundred talents were confiscated. With help, he escaped to Crete where one of his treacherous officers killed him. The money he left caused further troubles in Athens, for it was shown that Demosthenes and Demades had accepted bribes from it. When they couldn't pay their fine, they were exiled.

Alexander moved on to Opis after a short journey by river from Susa to the Persian Gulf. At Opis, intending to be considerate of the ageing soldiers in his army, he dismissed the old and infirm with a handsome sum. But the soldiers mutinied at what they again considered to be his intention of getting rid of them. The conflict arose while Alexander was explaining his beneficence to the troops. On hearing his plan to pension off the old soldiers, they took to raillery, with someone shouting 'Why not get rid of all the soldiers and march with your father' (a sarcastic reference to Ammon). Alexander broke off his talk and pointed to thirteen obstreperous soldiers, who were immediately marched to summary execution. In the stunned silence he rebuked the men with the speech in which he extolled the achievements of his father in bringing civilisation to Macedonia. He spoke of his own efforts to bring the country into world prominence.

But the troops were unmoved. Those not being pensioned off were equally rebellious at the thought of being left in the minority among Alexander's growing numbers of Persian troops. The king withdrew to his quarters, as he had done before, hoping they would change their minds. After two days there was no change. On the third day Alexander played his ace. He had it announced that his Companions would henceforth be Persians and only his Persian 'kinsmen' could kiss him. The Macedonians relented with this threat to their position in the army and in a tearful reconciliation Alexander declared, 'I make you all my kinsmen.'

The original intention to pension off Macedonians was carried through in great numbers, for eleven thousand men were to be sent home, enriched with extra pay and the tremendous sum of one talent for each of them. This may have been a calculated inducement for others to enlist, but Alexander had also taken the precaution of keeping all the children born of native women to raise them as good Macedonian soldiers. Before leaving, a huge feast for nine thousand celebrated the new era with Macedonians, Greeks and Persians all sharing Alexander's prayer for 'harmony and partnership'.

Craterus was appointed to escort the pensioners home. He was also charged with replacing Antipater as Viceroy and instructing Antipater to join Alexander. This change-over was by far the more significant act, since the viceroy had for so many years exercised independent power in Greece and Macedonia. Olympias had long counselled her son to get rid of Antipater and there can be no doubt that Antipater's power rivalled Alexander's. Craterus' progress towards Macedonia was very slow, raising the suspicion that he feared a confrontation with Antipater, if indeed the viceroy did intend to resist the orders. On the other hand, Antipater had just now, in 323, sent his son to Alexander, which surely no rebel would have done.

Following the Persian practice, Alexander retired with his troops to Ecbatana for the summer. It was a time of prodigious celebration, with games, feasts and drinking that befitted not only the Great King of Persia but also the climax of a legendary military campaign. At one of these debaucheries, Hephaestion collapsed. His condition got worse. He lingered several days with a high fever, but when Alexander was called to his bedside from one of the daily sporting events, his closest companion and friend was dead.

The king's grief was not placated when Hephaestion's doctor was executed or when all the sacred fires in the empire were extinguished. The body was embalmed and a funeral cortège was assembled to take the body to Babylon.

Alexander never fully recovered from mourning. The drinking continued in Babylon and the expedition to Arabia was mapped, with ships sent out on reconnoitring missions.

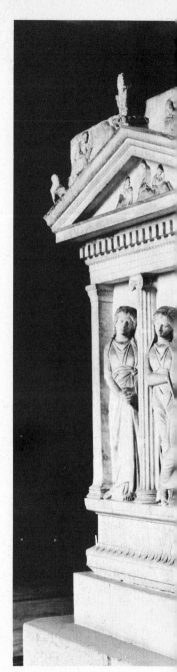

In the latter part of the nineteenth century Turkish
excavators at Sidon found a royal cemetery comprising
seven tomb-chambers containing seventeen sarcophagi.
This one of high relief statues of weeping women was
found together with the 'Alexander Sarcophagus'.

A Hellenistic king-list from Babylon of 175 BC. The obverse, shown here is inscribed in Babylonian, beginning with the names of the Hellenistic kings of Mesopotamia up to the time of uninterrupted Arsacid rule.

After one drunken revelling, Alexander was on his way to bed when he was called into a smaller, private party. After quaffing a goblet of unmixed wine, he shouted in pain and had to be carried to bed. Poison was not suspected and has no foundation in fact. He too suffered a high fever, but for several days he carried on his sacrificial duties. When he could no longer leave his bed, the Macedonians thronged to the palace doors fearful that the king was already dead. He fought his illness for eleven days, but succumbed on the morning of 10 June 323.

It was a life on an epic scale. His immediate tribute was that no one could replace him and his empire collapsed into divisive wars, murders and intrigues. His successors came from his own troops, but as he had been admonished before setting forth so long ago in the spring of 334, he had no heir. His wife Roxane was pregnant, and Perdiccas, to whom Alexander gave the royal seal just before dying, tried to hold the empire together until the child was born. He could not, and what dreams and ambitions Alexander still had died with him.

He was first called 'great' by the Romans who had ambitions to match his. He inspired conquerors throughout history. Julius Caesar cried when he read that Alexander had died at the age of thirty-two, before he himself had achieved anything. Louis XIV attended masquerades as Alexander. Napoleon kept Alexander's history by his bed. Michelangelo laid out the Vatican courtyard in the design of Alexander's shield. In his own day, news soon reached Athens that Alexander had died. The politician Demades tried to convince the people that it could not be true, 'for,' he said, 'if Alexander were really dead, the stench of the corpse would by now have filled the world'.

Select Bibliography

The earliest extant source on Alexander was written some three hundred years after his death. It was done by Diodorus Siculus as part of his 40-volume *Library of History*, of which Books 16 and 17 become increasingly involved with Macedonia and Alexander. C.Bradford Welles provides a fine translation and notes in the Loeb edition of Diodorus (1963), vol. 8. The most authoritative ancient source is Arrian, who wrote his *Anabasis* in the second century AD primarily as a literary exercise. He begins his narrative with Alexander's first battle and limits himself to military subjects. The translation of Aubrey de Selincourt has been revised and given notes by J. R. Hamilton, now published as *The Campaigns of Alexander* (Penguin, 1971).

Of the ancient sources, Plutarch's is the most readable and flattering. He takes the opposite tack from Arrian and concentrates on anecdotal insights into Alexander's character. Some anecdotes are obviously apocryphal, but Plutarch reports it all as though it were fact, an approach he staunchly defends: 'Just as painters seek the likeness of their subjects in the face and in the appearance about their eyes, wherein character is revealed, paying little attention to the rest of their bodies, so I must be permitted to enter more deeply into the indications of inner personality and . . . leave the grandeurs and struggles for others to describe.' The recent Penguin edition translated by Ian Scott-Kilvert, called *The Age of Alexander* (1973), includes eight biographies besides Alexander's. Those of Phocion and Demosthenes give an insight into contemporaneous reactions to the exploits of the man who overshadowed his age. Quintus Curtius fluctuates between heroic flattery and hostility in his portrait of Alexander (Loeb, 2 vols.), making his the least trustworthy of ancient sources.

Modern standard biographies tend to show great deference to Alexander as an example of strong, forceful leadership. Alexander studies in Britain inevitably refer to the work of W. W. Tarn, whose two-volume biography consists of a narrative and then numerous articles on aspects of Alexander's life (Cambridge University Press, 1948; Boston: Beacon Press, 1956). The standard German biography by Ulrich Wilcken comes in a Norton paperback edition translated by G. C. Richards. The notes by Eugene N. Borza are admirably up to date and scholarly, showing just how many discrepant sources there are, especially for facts like the number of soldiers at a particular battle.

Modern scholars, like Professor Borza, have shown admirable

restraint and care in the study of Alexander. Two compendia of modern scholarship show the state of Alexander studies in various aspects of his life: G. T. Griffith, ed., *Alexander the Great: The Main Problems* (Cambridge: Heffer, 1966), and the 'Alexander number' of *Greece and Rome* (vol. 12, No. 2, October 1965). Lionel Pearson's painstaking study, *The Lost Histories of Alexander the Great* (Bronx, New York: American Philological Association, 1960) pieces together the nature of the sources now available only through our ancient secondary sources. It is admirably complete, scholarly and readable. The work of E. E. Badian underpins the new research into the machinations of the Macedonian court before and during Alexander's reign. Some of his articles are gathered in *Studies in Greek and Roman History* (New York, 1964); further reference can be made to his own indispensable survey, 'Alexander the Great, 1948-67', in *Classical World* (vol. 65, Nos 2-3, October-November 1971). A summary of his view of Alexander is available in his two-part article in *History Today* (vol. 8, Nos 6 and 7, June and July 1958).

C. Bradford Welles in the posthumously published *Alexander and the Hellenistic World* (Toronto: A. M. Hakkert, 1970) devotes only one-fifth of the book to Alexander himself, but the portrait he draws is straightforward and understanding without being blindly admiring. J. F. C. Fuller's *The Generalship of Alexander the Great* (London: Eyre & Spottiswoode, 1958) is eminently readable and shows through the logistics of Alexander's battles just what a great general he was. Of two recent biographies, J. R. Hamilton (*Alexander the Great*, London: Hutchinson, 1973) is sometimes overcondensed and stiffly academic, while Robin Lane Fox (*Alexander the Great*, London: Allen Lane, 1973) tends toward romanticising, though his big book brings out much of the culture and geography of the areas Alexander marched through.

R. N. Frye's *The Heritage of Persia* (London: Weidenfeld & Nicolson, 1962) and Mortimer Wheeler's *Flames over Persepolis* (London: Weidenfeld & Nicolson, 1968) make good introductions to the areas Alexander conquered and his impact on them.

Acknowledgements

Photographs and illustrations were supplied or are reproduced by kind permission of the following:
Acropolis Museum, Athens, 46; Agence Rapho, 192–3; Archeological Museum, Salonika, 190; Ashmolean Museum, 67; British Museum, *3*, 18, 19, 20, 23, 39, 40, *52*, 59, 72–3, 75, 88, 94, 96–7, 104, 105, 129, 134–5, 137, *160*, 197, 201, 208, 209, 214; Camera Press, 128, 166; Deutsches Archäologisches Institut, Athens, 138; Dmitri, 10–11, *14–15*, 28–9, 30–1, 50, 56–7, 62, 71, 74, 120; Egyptian State Tourist Administration, 130; Freya Strak, 108; Hermitage Museum, 172, 173, 182 (photographer C. M. Dixon); Hirmer Fotoarchiv, 119, 158, 213; Imperial Iranian Embassy, 150; Istanbul Museum, 123, 157, 169, 202; J. Allen Cash, 126, 131, *148*, 186–7; John Freeman Ltd., *157*; Josephine Powell, 178–9; J. Paul Getty Museum, 84, 87; Kunsthistorisches Museum, Vienna, *49*; Louvre, 94; Mansell Collection, 25, 43, 47, 69, 76–7, 80–1, 90–1, 143, 164–5; Metropolitan Museum of Art, Rogers Fund, 67, 166; Michael Holford, *64*; Middle East Archives, 115; Museo di Villa Giulia, Rome, 195; Museum of Fine Arts, Boston, 27; National Museum, Beirut, 51; National Museum, Naples, 110–11; National Museum, Toronto, 83; Nick Stournaras, 44; Novosti Press Agency, 174–5; Ny Carlsberg Glyptothek, 13; Courtesy of the Oriental Institute, University of Chicago, 147, 152; Peter Clayton, 180, 194; Roger-Viollet, 36–7, 150, 151; Roger Wood, 131, 189; Royal Geographical Society, 17, 171; Scala, 2, *61*, *98–9*, *110–11*, *145*; Seattle Art Museum, 24, 86, 102; Sonia Halliday, 116; Staatsbibliothek, Berlin, 93; Staatliche Museen, Berlin, 39, 67, 103; University of Mississippi, 24, *endpapers*; Vatican, 95.

Numbers in italic indicate colour illustrations

Picture research by Michele Mason
Maps drawn by Design Practitioners Limited

Index